Neuropathways to Love

A woman's guide to harnessing the power of the brain to attract an amazing relationship

Cinthia Dennis

Published by NLP Re-Patterning, San Francisco, CA

ISBN 9781731413338 (paperback)

First Edition

Dedication

This book could not have been made possible without all of the powerful women with whom I have had the pleasure of working in the F.L.I.R.T. Courses. Your dedication to your love lives and your motivation to find healthy relationships have been inspiring. I have learned just as much from you as you have in the courses. THANK YOU!

A special thanks to my NLP mentors, Carl Buchheit and Michelle Masters. Not only have they been amazing teachers, but they have also helped me revise my own deep-seated patterns in love and relationship, which has, in turn, helped me help over one thousand women and counting in their own quest for love.

Other special thanks to my love Alexander, who finally showed up because of the heart and brain work I did to call him to me. He continues to be my true partner as we pioneer into the new relationship paradigm together.

Contents

Who Is This Book For?

This book is for women who are frustrated with love and relationships and are ready to find amazing men. Maybe they have tried other self-help books, therapy, matchmakers or dating apps, but nothing seems to work. Or maybe they are just starting out in the dating world and happened upon this book. This is a whole new approach to attracting healthy love based in neuroscience, NLP and the way the brain runs patterns of belief and behavior. These patterns can either attract good partners or put up blocks to finding them. Worse yet, some of those limiting patterns cause women to keep picking bad partners or cause them to get their hearts broken over and over.

Many of the concepts in this book can be applied to all intimate relationships, straight or gay, and any gender or sexual orientation, because most of the concepts in this book are universal. However, the book was intended for straight women seeking intimate relationship with men, because that is the area I have experience and expertise with. There are some specific pitfalls when it comes to straight relationships between men and women that are addressed in this book. It is not intended to be exclusionary. If you identify with the LGBT community, I encourage you to still read this book and skip the chapters that don't apply to you as well as change all pronouns to reflect who you are.

How to Read This Book to Change Your Brain and Open Your Heart

Maneuvering the pitfalls and mysteries of dating and relationships is a complicated undertaking these days. You may be questioning yourself and wondering why things just never seem to work out. You are not alone. There is nothing wrong with you and I applaud you for doing something to help yourself.

Congratulations! I know that, because you are reading this, that you have taken the first step: Commitment to change. Commitment leads to action and action changes things. Also, taking action tells your subconscious that you are worth it. And you *are* worth it!

Did you know that most people, most of the time don't do anything to change their lives when they are stuck? Just by getting this book you are stating that you are in control of making your life better. However, simply owning the book isn't going to change anything for you. You must commit to reading it and doing the exercises. I suggest you set aside 10-20 minutes a day to read a chapter and do the following exercises. Setting aside that time for yourself every day starts the process of growth and change and puts it into motion. By doing this, you are sending a strong message to yourself that you are important, what you want is important, and you are committed to your goals and dreams of having the love life that you truly desire. When you commit to yourself it raises your level of self-esteem. We will talk more about this in later chapters. High self-esteem is crucial to having a healthy, loving relationship, and it is the number one thing that is attractive to men.

I suggest getting a notebook specifically for the exercises in this book as you will be referring back to previous exercises throughout. Again, I want to stress the importance of setting aside a certain amount of time each day to do the exercises. It is important to be consistent in order to have your brain patterns change.

There are a few mindsets that I find useful while reading this book:

*Be open to learning new methods

Try these new concepts on. If they don't work for you later, then throw them out. There might be suggestions in this book that push your edges, but it's when you are up against your edge that learning and growth happen. What we want is usually out of our comfort zone, so we need to go a little bit past where we are comfortable in order to get what we want. I recommend finding that place where you feel only slightly uncomfortable and don't traumatize yourself by going way past your edge. A little at a time is best. As you lean into your edge a little bit at a time, your edges begin to stretch and grow.

*Give it your all

How you do anything is how you do everything. If you give this book and the exercises everything you've got, you will be amazed by the impact it will have when you are out in the world with dating and relationships. The results you will see and experience after reading this book are directly proportionate to the amount of effort you put into the process.

*Make a commitment to yourself

Buying this book and starting the journey is a commitment to yourself already! And that is change because you are telling yourself that YOU matter and what you want matters. When you set time aside to read and do the exercises in this book, you are again telling yourself that you matter, and this will begin to change your self-esteem.

*Stay on the train

Some of the exercises in this book can be challenging, and they might bring up emotions that are difficult at times. When these issues arise, people tend to want to quit. Try to think of it this way: imagine that you are on a train to having the relationship that you want. If you just stay on the train (even if you are running backwards) you will eventually get to your destination. If you jump off the train, you will never get there.

*Be willing to stop making it hard

A lot of what this course entails is changing your mindset. So often the women that I work with have mindsets that insist, "relationships are hard." They tell me, "It is hard to find a good man," etc. When we have had ups and downs in love and relationships, and especially if we have gotten our hearts broken a few times, we often walk away from those experiences with the belief that this love thing is hard. But what if it wasn't? What if it was easy? What would it be like if you could, at least while reading this book, pretend that it was easy? I invite you to pretend and to make it fun for yourself.

*Notice that with risk comes reward

Things that we want that we don't yet have are usually outside of our comfort zone. And in order to reach them, you might have to take some risks. But in this case, a risk might just be something you have never tried or done before.

*Take action, even if you don't have all of the answers yet

The concepts in this book are all built on each other. Reading through this at times might feel like doing a jigsaw puzzle without the box top picture to look at. I encourage you to do the exercises even if it's not yet obvious as to how they all fit the bigger picture.

*Know that it is okay for you to have more and be more in your life

Sometimes, our limiting beliefs stop us from allowing bigger and better things to come into our lives. We will talk a lot about these beliefs in the book and begin to shift them. But for now, please know that you, as well as everyone in the world, deserve amazing lives and love!

My Promise to you:

Not only am I here to give you insight, information and exercises to solidify change, but I am holding a space for you in the vision of what you want even if you can't see it yet.

These are some of the common complaints I hear from the women I work with:

1. They don't know how to find the good guys.
2. They often pick men that aren't good for them.
3. They don't understand men and how men view relationships and intimacy.
4. They are stuck in limiting, painful patterns.
5. They tend to lose themselves in relationships.
6. They don't understand how to move a relationship from casual to committed.
7. They feel nervous and lack confidence around the men in whom they are interested.
8. They don't know how to communicate their needs.

If any of this resonates with you, then you are in the right place and this book will be an excellent resource for you. There are many reasons why this love life stuff can be difficult. In this book, you will begin to understand what creates a good, healthy relationship as well as really learning what it takes to pick a great partner and make the relationship last. You will discover what some of your hidden blocks might be on the road to love and how to move through them.

Welcome to this unique, proven system to help you attract your perfect partner and have the love you deserve in your life. This system is like no other program or self-help book because all the concepts and exercises are rooted in the principles of how your neurology works around self-esteem, confidence and self-limiting patterns when it comes to relationships and attraction. That is why this book is different because it won't just teach you what to do. It will help you go deeper into how your brain is working and change its patterns so you can have the love you deserve and desire. I am wishing you amazing love that feeds your soul.

I am so glad you are here!

My Story of Heartbreak and Love

You are not alone in your quest for healthy, happy love and relationships!

Many women have come to me seeking that exact thing. I am a NLP Practitioner (neuro-linguistic programming) as well as a relationship and dating mentor. Since 2005, I have had the pleasure of helping women to not only have unstoppable confidence in their relationships and dating experiences but also to find love in their lives that they never thought possible. These women's journeys while working with me individually and in the F.L.I.R.T. relationship courses have inspired this book.

My own story of love and pain has also inspired me to share this knowledge. In my dating and relationship journey, I have had every dating foible there is to experience: from picking the "wrong" guy over and over again, to not liking the ones that were good for me to staying in relationships way too long, to coming on too strong and scaring men off, to being so picky that no one could ever make the cut, to not being picky enough and ending up with some really toxic people. I have been cheated on and verbally abused and have had partners that withheld sex and affection. I have had broken engagements and a failed marriage. Whatever the scenario, the story always ended the same way. I was alone and felt like I was destined to be alone forever. I began to think there must be something really wrong with me and that no one good would ever love me. These experiences and feelings were so frustrating and painful that learning "how" to date and have healthy relationships became my hobby, so to speak. I studied everything I could find about love and relationships. I studied social dynamics and learned about the components that created passion, intimacy, and amazing relationships. I finally ended up doing a three-year program in NLP, where not only did I learn how the brain worked around love and relationships, but I also had my own brain re-wired, in a sense, so that I could stop the limiting patterns that I had been repeating over and over: patterns that sabotaged my hopes for true connection and healthy love.

I began to realize that my relationship issues had everything to do with myself and my agonizing beliefs about love and my self-worth. The problems in my relationships really stemmed from my inability to value who I truly was, and they caused me to compromise myself and end up with people who were also broken and not really available for the relationship that I had always hoped for. When I began to apply all that I had learned about healthy relationships and the dynamics between men and women to my own dating life, I learned to do the feminine dance of dating and it wasn't long before dating became fun instead of heartbreaking! My life began to change. The men that started to come into my life were strong and full of integrity. I began to fill my life up with so much of "me" and so much of my own joy, that I no longer *needed* a man to fulfill me. That is when **I was finally ready to meet my true partner.**

After having had hundreds of women come to me with the same issues and finding a step-by-step system that really works to get them on the right track to attracting and creating the kind of relationships that will support their higher selves, I wanted to share the path to success with all the women who I know that dream of something bigger for themselves!

Modern Love

Why is it that dating and romantic relationships seem so hard these days? Is it true that things were easier back in our parents' and even our grandparents' day? Back then, it seemed like everyone could find someone to marry and start a family with. It was just a given that it would happen. It didn't even seem to require much knowledge or skill. People got married young, had children quickly and stayed together until they died. Simple, right?

If it used to be so simple then why is it that now I end up working with countless women who are frustrated with dating and can't seem to find good partners? They are single way into their forties and beyond. They compare themselves to how things were in the past. They feel inadequate, and they often feel that there must be something wrong with them because they can't find this one thing that is supposed to be a given and that used to be so easy for their parents and grandparents.

It isn't that it was easier back then. However, the criteria for marriage was much different. The motivation for being in lasting love relationships has changed quite a bit throughout history. Marriage used to be a business contract of sorts. Women needed men to take care of them financially and men needed women to produce offspring and carry on their names or help them with the farm or family businesses. Relationships were much more about survival than they were about love and having shared interests. If you happened to love your partner in a romantic sense, that was just a cherry on top but it wasn't a requirement to marry someone. Occasionally, people did find shared interests and passion, but it wasn't the goal.

I remember interviewing my grandmother before she died so I could capture her oral history. I asked her how she had met my grandfather. The story was simple, to the point and lacked any sense of romance.

"I was standing outside of church when your grandfather pulled up in a new car. He lived in the next town over and was visiting a cousin of his at our church. He pulled up next to me and asked if I wanted to go for a ride. I said yes. We began spending time together after church on Sundays, and my parents agreed to it because he came from a good Dutch family. After the traditional six months, he asked me to marry him, after speaking to my father first of course, and I said yes. I had never dated anyone else, and it was time for me to get married as I was turning nineteen that year. We moved into the farmhouse on his uncle's property where your grandpa was working. I had your aunt Ruth a year later."

"Grandma, how did you know you were in love with Grandpa? How did you know he was the one?" I asked her.

"He was the one because he showed up and he was a good Christian and came from a good Dutch family. That is how I knew. What kind of silly question is that?"

And there you have it. My grandmother continued to call me up throughout my twenties and ask me if I had met any good, Christian, Dutch gentlemen. If that was the only criteria, my love life would have been much simpler considering I grew up in a mostly Dutch, Christian community.

It was much easier to pick a partner when your criteria was that limited. You didn't necessarily need to get along with this person and have similar interests. Your similar interest was survival, and that was all that mattered. You became teammates for survival.

Life was actually harder back then, so all energy went to making sure you were able to make it. With that being the focus, asking oneself whether or not one was happy just was out of the question.

When life became more industrialized and therefore easier, survival-focused relationships eventually gave way to the concept of romantic love. Once women could survive on their own, work and make money, and didn't really need men anymore, romantic love became more of a desire. We were spoon-fed the concepts of romantic love through books and movies. The idea that you will find your soul mate and he will always love you and totally under-stand you is what has screwed a lot of women up. The concept that there is that one person out there for you and all you need to do is find him in order to live happily ever after has been the dangling carrot of love for a while now. This is what many women I know have been striving for. These women have fallen short over and over, leaving them feeling broken and defective. What if I told you that romantic love isn't what relationships are about either?

Yes, the juicy love chemicals that flood our brain when we first meet some-one are intoxicating and delicious. But it doesn't last. It isn't supposed to last. If we no longer need men for survival, can be rock stars in the business world, can get sperm donors to have children without them and realize that romantic love juices never last, then what are we really looking for?

I would like to propose that one of the reasons why people are finding it so difficult these days to find good partners is because they are operating in an old paradigm that no longer holds true for our modern society. We are falling short because we don't know what we really want and we are not satisfied with our choices because we are looking at it all wrong. When you don't NEED to be in a relationship then ask yourself this: what DO you want by being in one?

A journey begins with a clear vision of where you want to go. I would like to suggest a new way of looking at intimate relationships. What if relating and being with romantic partners was seen as a spiritual path and a personal growth opportunity for both people to see themselves clearly? If both people could see the truth of who they are, to see where those tender wounds are that need love and attention. What if the point was to learn how to relate to others and ourselves at the same time?

A relationship is a playground to explore, be curious, and play with the concepts of love and acceptance of others and ultimately of yourself. Imagine if children approached a playground with the same seriousness that most people approach love. What if they took every skip and turn around on the merry-go-round with a heavy attitude? What if every time their side of the teeter totter was down, they made it mean something was wrong with them? Intimate relationships are an important part of being human, but maybe they aren't as serious and dire as we make them out to be. When we use the old models of looking at them, like, "I have to find someone or I won't survive." Or "I have to find romance or I am not lovable and I am broken," then it takes all the fun out of what can really be happening.

In reality, people come into our lives. Some stay and some go. Everyone is here to hold a mirror up to you so you can do the work you need to do. Why not make it a fun trip this time? Why not make it a playful adventure this time? Why not just have fun this time? Relationships naturally go through ups and downs. Why not set the goal of what you ultimately want to have and reverse engineer it?

For instance, if your goal is to open your heart as much as you can to someone, then you will find yourself with experiences that might open your heart or give you challenges to push you beyond your current limits with vulnerability. If your goal is to find a partner who inspires you to be the best version of yourself and you them, the flavor of your experiences might look different from your friends' and families' experiences.

The point is that you can be and do anything this time around. It is your reality, it is your life. What do YOU want?

I sat down and asked myself why I felt the need to write this book. The answer that came to me was this: People need to know that they aren't failures if their relationships aren't working out. You aren't broken if you can't seem to create the same family life as your mother or grandmother did. In your soul, you know you want more out of life then they were able to have. You are on a different journey. Your soul craves more than what you may have currently experienced. I want you to know that you are beautiful and lovable just as you are. I want you to be able to craft a life that feeds your soul. A loving relationship isn't a separate piece, but it is integral to the whole human experience. If you have been frustrated with this for a while now, it means that you are a forerunner to the next evolution of what a relationship can be. This is your guide to create something unique for yourself. It doesn't have to match what your friends are doing or what society says needs to happen. It is just for you. And *thank you* for moving our society forward to the next phase, where we can break out of the oppressive molds that love has been put in.

You don't need to look towards your family for your model relationship. You don't need to look towards movies and popular culture. All you need to do is look inside of yourself and become clear and healthy within yourself, and you will find your perfect match.

1

The Map
"Knowing Where You Are and Knowing Where You Want to Go"

In this chapter, you will get a very clear idea of where you are presently in regards to relationships, where you have been and where you want to go. This is a very important step in finding the kind of love that is right for you. Many women who I work with have no idea what they are looking for when it comes to a relationship. Because of that, they waste their time with men who are not well suited for them. Unfortunately, they learn this the hard way by getting attached to someone just to find out that it will not work out or make them happy.

First, let's be clear about where you are now. Before you move forward, you need to know where you are currently so you can see a clear path towards where you are headed. If a friend called you up and asked for directions to your house, in order to steer him or her in the right direction, the first thing that you would need to know is *where are you now?*

EXERCISE:
Where are you now and where have you been?

1. Take a moment and write about what it has been like for you in your past and/or current love relationships. What is happening now? What has

happened in the past? What are your frustrations and how have you felt about it?

_____

_____

_____

_____

_____

2. Have you noticed any themes or patterns in your relationships or dating life? Sometimes, things can appear to be different but we are left feeling similar. The feelings we are left with can also be a pattern.

_____

_____

_____

_____

_____

3. What have been some of the main emotions you have felt in your relationships?

_____

_____

_____

_____

_____

4. What would you like to move away from in relationships?

_____

_____

_____

_____

EXERCISE:
Where do you want to go?

So often we don't really know specifically what we want but we are clearer about what we *don't* want. Or sometimes we are focused on the pain of not having what we want. For years, I have been working with my clients to get their brains to cooperate with their goals. They are often focusing on how much it sucks being single and try to move away from that feeling. But when they are focusing on what they don't want, they just get more of the same.

Answering these questions will help you to become clearer about your goal:

1. What **would** you like now in a relationship? I will give you permission to be unreasonable. Meaning, often we limit ourselves in what is possible because of our past experiences. If you could design the perfect relationship for yourself, **what would you want?**

   _____

   _____

   _____

   _____

   _____

2. How will it **feel** when you have what you want in a relationship? What are the main emotions that go with having what you want?

   _____

   _____

   _____

   _____

3. What would you be **doing** differently?

_____

_____

_____

_____

_____

4. What would the relationship **look** like?

_____

_____

_____

_____

_____

Give your brain clear messages of what you want

It is important to give your brain a clear picture of what you want in a relationship. The brain responds the same way to everything you tell it. Whether you are focused on what you want or what you don't want, your brain will always set out to create what you are focusing on.

Have you ever thought to yourself, "Why don't I have what I want even though I am working really hard to get it?" Your conscious mind might be working really hard, but it is the visionary of your life, not the worker bee. It really isn't in charge of making things happen. The subconscious is in charge of going out and getting what we want in life. Your subconscious can only attract what it concludes and it only has the capacity to make conclusions based on what you tell it to do. It does not make any decisions on its own. It only concludes what is true, based on what we tell it on a daily basis. Yet, the subconscious is a powerful agent in getting and having what we want in life.

Sometimes it feels like it is always giving us what we DON'T want; however, that is only because we are telling it the wrong things or giving it mixed messages and not being clear.

Think of your subconscious as if it were a good soldier that only follows orders from you. It always says yes to whatever we tell it. But, like a child, it takes everything literally and does not see through the contradictions that we often tell it. It doesn't hear the subtleties of what we mean. It only hears what we say and think to ourselves or say out loud.

The subconscious will always agree with what we tell it and then set itself to the task of making what we tell it real and true for us in the outside world. For example: Let's say someone (we'll call her Jane) decided she was ready for a lasting, loving relationship. Jane's subconscious would then say, "Yes, let's go find that. Your wish is my command." Then let's say Jane starts to think about the process of finding that special someone and she hits some bumps along the way. She might start to say to herself, "Good men are hard to find." Jane's subconscious then says, "Yes, they are hard to find. Your wish is my command. Let's make them hard to find." After some time, Jane might start to feel like she isn't meant to have what she wants: "Maybe I am not meant to have a good relationship." Her subconscious then says, "Yes, you must not be meant to have that." Then it will go ahead and make sure that these things are true by only letting experiences that match the thoughts come in or register.

As you start to understand this concept, you will realize just how much control you really do have in your life to achieve and obtain what you want. The first step in harnessing the power that you already have within you is to be very careful about what you think and feel. What is also important in using the power of your mind is to only focus on the end result rather than the process of HOW to achieve what you want. This way you won't get tripped up on all the negative thinking that might come up around how hard it might be to obtain. Also, it leaves the ways in which your desires and goals can manifest much more open instead of narrowing it down to only one specific path. It is similar to being a good boss. A good boss will have a clear vision and then trust his or her employees to get the job done rather than worrying about HOW it will happen.

Another key ingredient in using your mind to manifest your desired relationship successfully is to suspend your limiting beliefs about what is possible. While envisioning your ultimate goal as if it has already manifested, try to believe that there is nothing in the way of it really happening. Beliefs are the only things that get in the way of having everything that we want.

We will always get what we believe is possible or true about ourselves or the world. The funny thing about beliefs is that they are conclusions our brain made up usually a long time ago, but they are not necessarily true. Our life experiences are then filtered and distorted to match the beliefs that already exist in our minds, thus becoming feedback loops which then strengthen our beliefs. We will talk more about these limiting beliefs later in the book. In the meantime, try to envision what you want in love and suspend any limiting beliefs about it happening.

Are you going towards what you want or moving away from where you are?

There are two main motivation styles that our brains will use to obtain goals or desires. Whether it is getting projects done, creating your five-year plan or embarking upon dating and love, people tend to use the same motivation style on everything they do.

Away from motivation is when your brain focuses on avoiding something you don't want or focusing on how bad things feel to motivate you to do something to change it or "move away" from it. For instance, in the past, I would scare myself by picturing myself old and alone with no one around to take care of me or be with me in the future. This would be the motivation my brain used to convince me to go out and date so I could meet someone to circumvent my fears of being alone. It was a strong motivator! I would push myself to go out and meet people and to go on dates with people who I might not normally be interested in. I made a plan to thwart what my possible future was shaping up to be as a single spinster with 100 cats: "Go on as many dates as possible and marry the first person who asks."

The problem with this kind of motivation is that it kept me from finding what I really did want. I was so focused on my fear that I missed many red flags with the people I dated. When I met someone who showed a little bit of interest I would try and force it to work just so I would be safe from my fears of being alone. Eventually, these relationships would leave me feeling alone and sad anyway because I was forcing myself to be with people who I knew, deep down, were not a good fit for me.

Often, I see women motivated to find a partner because they are lonely or because they are afraid they won't get married or have children. They feel desperate and they want to find a relationship to make it better. The problem with this way of thinking is that the brain is designed to create what we focus on. If you are focusing on the pain, loneliness, and fear, then your brain will just create more pain, loneliness, and fear. It will do this either by picking partners who will leave you feeling that way or by sabotaging your plans and keeping you single so you will continue to feel that way. Remember, your brain is always saying yes to whatever you are focusing on and it will seek out experiences that will give you what it thinks you want. In this case, it would be more fear, more loneliness, and more pain.

People who have a *towards motivational style* focus on what they want, how good it will feel to get what they want, and what positive things it will do for them. Their desires become so juicy that it magnetizes the brain and pulls them towards it. There isn't a right or wrong way to execute motivation. In fact, both methods have their place in different situations. They both have their upsides and down-sides. For example, you hope that structural engineers who are designing bridges have an *away from* motivational style. In designing the bridges, their brains must be really good at noticing all the possible factors that can go wrong and take measures to prevent any potential disasters. This is definitely a good thing.

People who have the preferred method of *towards motivation* tend to go for what they want easily. They get energized and can start goals without much resistance. The downside to being a "towards" person is this: because these people tend to only look at the benefits of achieving or getting something, they sometimes forget to look for possible problems.

Even though both sides are good for what they are good for, when setting out to create a healthy relationship, utilizing a *towards* motivational style is the best. But this only applies once you get really clear about what you want to feel and what benefits you will get. Your loyal subconscious will know exactly what to go find. Not only that, but if you are focusing on what you want, then when something comes your way that doesn't match up to it, you will be much clearer about it NOT being the thing that is for you and won't miss the red flags. You will be more likely to avoid ending up in relationships that aren't good for you.

Setting your compass to find the love life you truly want

A compass is a device that keeps you from getting lost. The cool thing about a compass is that it is always right. It is infallible. It will always point north. Wouldn't it be great if you had such a compass when it came to love and dating? What if you could be on a date and pull the compass out of your purse to check to see if he was a good fit for you? That would save so much time and energy. Or what if you had been dating someone for a while and you were in that uncertainty phase, wondering whether or not he was going to be relationship material? Instead of complaining to your girlfriends and trying to get them to tell you whether you should leave or wait it out, what if you just knew what to do without a doubt? If you are looking at your love life as a map leading from where you are now to where you would like to be, what do you use as your compass to guide your way?

In the past, the women I work with have made lists of what they want in a man. They felt that if only they could clarify exactly what they wanted, then Mr. Right would magically appear. However, the way they were making their lists would actually limit who or what could come into their lives. Not only would the lists prevent these women from giving Mr. Right a chance, but they were also keeping them from recognizing Mr. Wrong.

Their lists would look a lot like this:

I want a man who is 6 feet tall with brown hair and blue eyes.
I want him to be rich.
I want him to drive a nice car.
I want him to take me to expensive restaurants.
I want him to want children.
I want him to love me unconditionally.
I want him to be responsible.
etc.

I know, I know. I also used to have a list similar to this. Before I discovered how to work with my neurology to pick good partners, I had a long list of very specific qualities, looks, values and goals that my future partner needed to have. I figured if I was wishing, I was going to go for broke! I mean, if there is a Santa Claus that is bringing me my true love, I might as well get the top of the line model, right? In theory, this sounds like good advice, however, one of the backlashes to this kind of list is that women are ruling out amazing men just because they don't fit their limited list of specific qualifications. It is a delicate balance between knowing what you want and stating it and limiting yourself and your opportunities for love.

EXERCISE:
How do I want to feel? — Broadening your scope

For this next exercise, you are going to broaden your scope. You are going to make a different kind of list. This list will be specific, but it is going to focus on how you want to FEEL with your partner instead of external specifics. Really feeling good in a relationship is far more important than being driven around in a BMW.

In this next section, I am going to have you make your "how I want to feel list." Instead of writing "I want a six-foot tall, brown-eyed, blonde man," write something like: "I want to feel attracted to him physically and find him sexy." Or instead of writing "I want him to be rich," ask yourself, "What would I get out of him being rich?" For example, the answer might be "I want to feel taken care of."

When rewriting your list, be careful to not try and solve a problem. We often get clearer about what we want because of our past mistakes and getting what we didn't want. For example, if in the past you had a boyfriend who was always underemployed and struggling financially, you might later put on your list that your future partner needs to make a lot of money. You figure, well if he is making a lot of money then I won't have to go through that again. But making a lot of money could also entail being with someone who is a workaholic and not available to spend much time with you. Someone who makes a lot of money still might struggle because he is always afraid that he might lose the money. Also, wealthy people are not always generous with their money so it might not feel as secure as you are hoping. Instead, what if you wrote something like this: "I want to feel that my future partner and I are on the same page financially. I want to feel like there is abundance no matter how much money is coming in and I want to feel unburdened by finances—both his and mine." How would all of this make you feel?

The good thing about focusing on the feelings that you want to have is that you always have the ability to notice how you are feeling at any given moment. If you really start to trust your instincts, they will become louder and stronger. If you spend enough time clarifying how you want to feel in every aspect of your relationship and then start trusting your feelings, (*yes, I am feeling this* or *no, I am not feeling this*) then you will have a magic compass that is always with you, guiding you in your search for a strong, healthy relationship.

List how you would like to *feel* in your ideal relationship:

_____

_____

_____

_____

_____

_____

_____

_____

_____

_____

Seek what you want within first

There is a trap to seeking what we want in a partner based on things that we lack in ourselves. For instance, let's say you want to find a partner who inspires your creativity but you yourself are a stuck artist. Remember what you radiate is like a magnet and will pull more of that to you. For example, if you are floundering in your life and having a hard time organizing and keeping on top of things and you think that finding an organized partner will help straighten things out, think again. This is what we call codependence. Not only will it not work to find someone to save or fix where you yourself are stuck, but it is unfair of you to require that from someone else. Be who you want to find first. If you need your financial life cleaned up, do it before you seek partnership. If you feel stagnant and stuck in life, figure out ways to un-stick yourself before you look for your partner or you will either end up finding stuck people or repelling men who are inspired and motivated in their life. The worst case would be that you find someone who needs to save you to feel good about himself, which means you will always need saving in one way or another in order for him to stick around.

Ruling out the good guys

*Joan was a participant in the F.L.I.R.T. Course a while back. She was a woman in her fifties who had been single for almost 12 years! When she enrolled in F.L.I.R.T. she was about to give up on love altogether. She had been on an enormous number of dates but said she could never find a good guy. She kept adding on to this very long list of things she wanted her future partner to have because she figured if she was really clear about what she wanted, it would manifest before her. Her list kept growing and growing. After exploring her list in class, we came to realize that her number-one top priority, a non-negotiable item on the list, was that her future partner MUST have a doctorate's degree. I asked her what she had hoped to gain from being with someone who had a doctorate's degree, and she simply stated that then they would be able to have intelligent conversations. You see, Joan was a professor and a scientist. She was intelligent and sharp. In the past, she had a hard time feeling fulfilled with the men she was dating because they weren't able to have smart conversations with her or inspire her. After exploring this a little further, she began to realize that maybe just putting "we can have intelligent conversations" on the list vs. **how** she thought that might be accomplished would really open up who might actually be a good partner for her.*

She also began to realize that just because someone had a high educational degree, it didn't necessarily make him a good conversationalist. After examining how she felt when she was being stimulated intellectually, Joan was able to reset her compass. When she went out on dates after that, she could check in with herself to see if she was feeling intellectually stimulated or not. Since she was no longer interviewing her dates based on their credentials, she was able to meet a wonderful man within two months of changing her list with whom she really clicked, both emotionally and intellectually. He didn't even have a doctorate's degree.

The Brain Distorts Reality

Another advantage to creating your relationship compass and setting it to how you want to FEEL is that quite often our brain distorts reality. When we really want to be in a relationship, it is difficult to see the men before us very clearly. When we aren't seeing people clearly, we can end up with people and situations that are not good for us and are not at all what we want.

The beauty of the "feeling" list is that the way you feel is always with you and is more reliable than whether or not someone is driving a nice car or has a good job. We often look at the subjective things about a person's life and make them mean certain things about a person's character, but our interpretations are not always correct.

If you get really clear about how you want to feel before you go out into the world of dating, then you will always have a reliable compass with you, pointing you in the right direction so you don't get lost.

We all have "gut instincts" and I would say that these instincts are usually spot on. The question is are you listening to yourself? Men are much better at trusting and listening to their instincts. Women, on the other hand, will often rationalize their feelings away. They don't trust themselves, and therefore will come up with reasons and excuses. They question why they feel something or they make rationalizations for other people's behavior.

How did I not see that he was Mr. Wrong?

Kim was a high-powered executive. Because she was so good at taking control and getting things done, she had a difficult time finding men who could be strong enough around her. She deeply wanted a high-powered man in her life to take over so she could relax, and she had a hard time finding such a man until she met Steven.

Steven had an amazing job. He was in control, decisive and commanded respect. He had exquisite tastes and when he met Kim, he was very proactive in pursuing her. This was exactly what she had always wanted in a man. He made plans to take her to expensive restaurants and high society events. He bought her jewelry and sent her flowers. She was in heaven, and it felt like she had finally met her match. A few months later, things went very wrong. Steven's taking control, planning things and having a strong direction, which Kim had thoroughly enjoyed in the beginning, started to turn into more than she had bargained for. He began to dictate what she could do or not do when he wasn't around. She was never allowed her own opinion about anything. It actually began to feel quite scary and if she hadn't ended it, it might have turned abusive. You see, Kim had felt a little uneasy the whole time with Steven, but she was so excited to finally be with a man who could make decisions that she ignored her instincts. On her list, she had things like "must have a good high-powered job," "strong personality," "spends money on me." All these things were true of Steven, but if she had paid attention to how she wanted to feel instead, she might not have picked him. When exploring this, she realized that what she really wanted to feel is that she was "being cared for," "respected," and "able to relax." None of these were really happening with Steven.

Learning to trust yourself

The art of learning to trust yourself comes with practice. Your inner voice has always been there, but if you have continually disregarded it, you have not developed the trust cycle that you need.

If you have often defaulted to what others tell you is right and have not strengthened your own intuition muscle, then your compass will be weak at first. Maybe you have made mistakes in the past and instead of learning from them, you have just decided not to trust yourself.

The best way to strengthen this muscle is to listen to your instincts carefully without questioning them. This might be tricky at first if you are in the habit of questioning yourself, but the more you just listen to yourself, the more your inner voice will be heard clearly.

I recommend acknowledging your first instinct on things and proceeding to act upon it without question and without having to have a reason or justification for it. This kind of trust in yourself will build your compass muscle and turn up its volume. The more you trust it the more it will become trustworthy.

For example, let's say you have gotten really clear on how you want to feel with your future partner. Let's pretend that one of the things you yearn for the most is the feeling of being seen and understood. You can imagine what that feels like, right? Then you go on a date with a man who is continually distracted on his phone, doesn't ask you any questions about yourself and doesn't seem like he cares to know you at all. If he asked you out for a second date and you were clear about your compass, you would automatically say, "No thank you." You wouldn't have to make excuses or justifications for your answer. You would just say no without giving it a second thought. This will build trust between you and your instincts.

On the other hand, let's say you were out with a man who was attentive and curious about you. Those feelings of being seen and understood might start to match up and you would already know that if he asked you out again, you could trust a *yes* instinct.

Do you want to date the moon or the sun?

I love looking at the moon. It is mysterious and beautiful. It is often thought of as feminine in essence. The other thing that is interesting about the moon is that it doesn't generate its own light. It only reflects the light of the sun. Depending on where it is in relation to the sun it will show up as full, half, slivers or not at all. Basically, without the sun, we couldn't even see it.

There is a kind of man who you need to be aware of if you want a truly equal and fulfilling relationship. I call them moon men. They are the men who don't have their own drive, energy, motivation or light. When women who are driven, energetic, have a zest for life and are passionate about something find themselves with moon men, they end up feeling frustrated, drained and bored. These women are generating the sun energy and the moon men are draining them in order to shine. Moon men don't generate their own light. They look for strong women to orbit around in hopes to boost their own energy.

If you identify with sun energy, you might want to ask yourself if you are attracting other suns or if you have moons orbiting around you? The healthiest relationships occur when two people contribute equally to the vibrancy in the relationship. They are both shining and positively influencing each other. How do you know when someone is a moon?

Here are some ways to tell:

*   They rarely have ideas about what to do and often rely on you to make the plans.
*   They don't have much going on in their lives and aren't passionate about much.
*   They don't have their own purposes in life outside of you.
*   They don't influence you in a positive way or inspire you to respect them.

By the way, respect is a much higher emotion than loving someone. The spark will soon fade if you don't respect and admire someone. If you are finding yourself with moons rather than suns, ask yourself, "What do you get out of being with moons?" The answer might surprise you.

Back in the day, I would continue to be frustrated over and over in my relationships. I had the nagging feeling that things were out of balance. I felt like I was giving a lot and the people I was with were happy doing the taking. I would find men who gravitated towards me because they felt pulled to do their own healing work. Subconsciously or not, they wanted and needed someone to help them grow. This in itself is not a bad thing. However, as it turned out, I was grooming these men so they would be better partners to their next girlfriends. These immature, failure-to-launch, commitment phobic, self-centered dudes would often find themselves getting married and having wonderful relationships not long after we broke up. Why? Because being with me was a stepping stone for them to grow up and become the sort of men and partners who healthy women would want to marry.

At first, I thought this meant that maybe I just wasn't enough for them and that is why they wouldn't grow up and show up for me. But after the third time this happened, I began to realize that I was picking moon men. I realized I had a lot to give someone. I was passionate about things I was doing in my life, I was driven and I was doing a lot of work on myself to grow and heal. The difference was this was all self-directed. I was doing these things for myself. I was sun energy. The imbalance I felt in my relationships was because I was with men who weren't their own suns. They were pulling on my energy to jump start their own lives.

There are times—even if you are with another sun—that you might need to rely on your partner to inspire you every once in a while, and vice versa. This is healthy and good. It becomes unhealthy when you are both stuck in the roles of either leader and fixer or broken and needy. A healthy relationship has a balance of energy being given and taken. These moon men didn't have much to offer me in return as far as my own growth and inspiration. So, I was left feeling resentful and not really knowing why.

If you are a sun, you need to be with another sun. Can you imagine the powerful sparks that will propel both of you forward when your partner is motivated to move forward in his life and you are in yours? When two suns get together they pull each other forward. When a sun energy is with a moon there is a continuous drag. You might feel like you need to pull him forward so you can keep going.

The other thing to ask yourself is if **you** fall into the moon category? Are you looking for suns to help you because you aren't generating your own light? If so then I hate to tell you, but you will become a drag and burden on your partner eventually.

Jody was a successful career woman. She had her life together and was also committed to her creative and personal growth. When she met Tom, he presented himself as a sensitive and caring man. He was interested in what she was doing as far as her business ventures and her meditation practices. He was a late bloomer as far as career and lifestyle, but his openness to her way of doing things in life felt promising. Not only that, but his interest in the details of her life felt like he really wanted to get to know her and that felt great.

Later, his charming interest in her small business and how she saw the world and spirituality started to feel draining. He would continually turn their conversations to these things in her life. She began to realize that his interest in these things wasn't to get to know her. Rather, he wanted to pull himself out of the stagnant life he had been living and also wanted to learn how to do that from Jody. The energy between them began to feel very unbalanced, and Jody started to feel resentful that Tom wasn't really bringing anything of his own to the table. He had put her in the teacher role without asking her. Jody also admitted that at first, she liked teaching him things. It made her feel useful. But such an imbalance gradually eroded any sexual chemistry she had with him and she eventually had to end it.

Finding your equal

I can't stress enough how important it is to find your equal partner. If you go for men who aren't doing as well as you financially, spiritually, emotionally, intellectually or if they are simply not going forward in their life, I guarantee that you will be dissatisfied eventually. You will become resentful when they aren't keeping up with you. It will begin to feel like they are holding you back. You will either become silently resentful or you will become the world's biggest nag in hopes that they get their lives together so you can move forward with them.

When you are in a partnership with someone, don't be fooled. Whatever they are doing or not doing in their life WILL affect you, even if you are an independent person. For example, let say you marry a man who isn't very good with his finances and you are responsible about yours. The time comes when you want to buy a house. He agrees, yes, that would be a great idea! But when it comes down to it, he blows his extra money on unnecessary things instead of saving for a down payment. Moreover, you come to find out he has a terrible credit score and there goes the house buying plan.

What about personal growth and emotional maturity? Let's say you are a person who is committed to growth, change and overcoming some of your challenges, and yet your partner doesn't have the same desires. He may see his challenges but either he complains about them or he doesn't even try to move past them because he doesn't feel in control of his own experience. What will happen then? You will most likely outgrow him or you will become bogged down by trying to help him get unstuck so once again, YOU can move forward.

What's love got to do with it?

Love. Isn't it what we are all looking for? Someone to love. Someone to love us back. This is an important part of being human and being fulfilled. Love is a need just like food and shelter. But LOVE is not enough when it comes to a sustainable relationship. If you don't feel this one very important thing towards your partner, it either won't last or you'll both end up miserable together.

I am talking about RESPECT. Respect is just as important as love in a relationship. You can love your partner and not respect him. But I am telling you, neither of you will be truly happy in the relationship unless you respect him.

The kind of respect I am talking about is the kind where you absolutely, totally admire him. The kind where you glance over at him and you think, "Wow, what a great guy." Or when you look up to the choices and decisions that he makes and admire the way he carries himself through life.

So often women love their partners but deep down inside they don't respect them. They don't like how they live their lives or the choices that they make and secretly they want their partners to change. These women might try and get their partners to eat better, wear better clothes, take care of their apartments and pay their bills on time. They push, they nag, and when that doesn't work, they will scream at their partners to do better. Sound familiar?

I am not blaming you for yelling and nagging. I know what is really happening behind the resentment and frustration. You want your man to own up, stand up and be in his masculine energy. You want him to be a man who you admire and respect because that is the only way you will ever trust him. And by trust, I mean that you can fully relax and lean into him because they know that he's got it taken care of. You want to trust his decisions and you don't want to feel the need to micromanage him, so you can RELAX into being in your feminine energy: Flow, creativity, love, softness, and lack of concern. We will talk more about feminine and masculine essence later.

Even though I understand why women nag, I will say this: If you find yourself in situations over and over where you feel like you can't trust your guy or you don't admire and respect him then ask yourself:

"Why do I keep picking men who disappoint me?"

Why are you picking men who you already know don't have their sh#$ together?

If you are picking men in the hopes that they will live up to their full potential even though they aren't doing that yet, then you have no one else to blame but your faulty picker.

It is the most dangerously disappointing thing to fall in love with potential. I am not saying that people don't grow and change. We all do, naturally, to some extent. But men rarely change because someone tells them to, or more accurately, nags them to do it.

Every person you pick should have an "As Is" sticker on them like used cars often do. That means, what you see is what you get. If you can't live with what you see, don't fool yourself into thinking that you can just fix him up to be what you want. It is best to start with someone who is already what you want.

Here are some examples of things women often complain about and try to get their man to change:

He doesn't make plans.
He forgets things.
He doesn't follow through with his promises.
He lies.
He defers all decisions to you.
He doesn't have his life together or doesn't take care of himself.
He doesn't have a healthy lifestyle.
He plays too many video games.
He watches porn.
He is messy.
He is underemployed.
He is bad with his finances.
He doesn't have goals or dreams.

Not only do these things create frustration, but they also force a woman to be in her masculine energy.

Ask yourself: Can I live with it?

If he doesn't make plans?
If he is irresponsible?
If he isn't taking care of himself?
If he flakes on his promises?
If he lies?
If he watches too much T.V.?
If he eats pizza and junk food?
If he is inactive?
If he is messy?
If he is bad with money?
If he doesn't seem to have the motivation to have a better life?

If the answer is "Yes, I can live with it," then you can't whine about it, and you can't push or nag him. You truly have to accept him as is. If the answer is "No, I can't accept it," then you have two options:

1. Leave and pick a more mature, masculine man.
2. Step back and stop doing everything in the relationship. See if he picks up the slack. If not, then you have your answer. Sometimes women step in and take over so much that it polarizes men to be even more passive. Stop making all of the decisions, the healthy meal planning and the stealth ideas of getting him to be more active and see what happens. If he still doesn't step up (after a reasonable time—you have to give him time to get untrained) then refer to Option #1.

I know this sounds harsh, but it isn't fair to yourself to settle for something that will be more disappointing than fulfilling, and it isn't fair to him to keep harassing him to be different. You get the picture. Nothing will get a woman more riled up than when she feels forced to be in her masculine energy in a relationship, and this occurs when she doesn't trust that her man will take care of business. It will make you more resentful than you know. Then you will nag, nag, nag. You secretly despise him for robbing you of your right to relax and he will secretly resent you for belittling him. And then, say bye-bye to passion and sex.

It could be that you are picking weak men and then wanting them to be strong. This is about as logical as getting a cat and then getting mad because it won't play fetch or go on walks with you. Or it could also be that you are so used to calling the shots and need so much control in your life that you never give him a chance to make decisions. Maybe you take over because you are too afraid to give up the wheel. If that is the case, we need to look at what is going on with you that you can't let go. If you have a hard time giving up control, you might be subconsciously picking weak men. And if this is the case, it will be useful to explore this later in the beliefs chapter.

EXERCISE:
What do you respect?

1. What gets you to respect the man you are with?

   _____

   _____

   _____

   _____

   _____

2. What do you need to see happen for you to admire him?

   _____

   _____

   _____

_____

_____

Can you imagine a version of you in the future in a relationship with a man whom you not only love but you also think is amazing? What would it be like to be proud that he is your partner? Imagine looking over at him and wanting to be a better person because he is so inspiring to you.

All couples argue and fight sometimes. Right? Now imagine yourself having a disagreement or a fight with this man. But you still totally think he is amazing. How do you think the argument will pan out?

Now imagine that you are in a relationship with a man who, in your opinion, is always screwing up. You think he has a lot of room for improvement. Now let's say you get into a disagreement with this guy. How does it feel when you already have some harbored resentments and disapproval going on? How do these two different scenarios play out?

I married my shadow

After my husband and I got divorced, due to financial circumstances, I had to stay in the same house with him for over a year after we split. It was only the San Francisco housing crisis that kept us stuck us together even after our relationship came unglued.

This was fortunate in a way because I had to reconcile my resentment towards him. I was stuck with him, and living with someone who you hate is no fun. I had to figure out a way to be okay with him and to be okay with how our relationship had fallen apart. I had to look at my part in the breakdown and the reasons why I had picked him in the first place. Most people, after they split up, never get to have that healing experience with the other person because they get to just walk away. They may never have to face it again, but it doesn't mean it doesn't stick with them and haunt them. It can sometimes even ruin their chances of future love.

We had to come to a place of peace with each other. After many nights of processing what went wrong, how I had felt and how he had felt, with tears and genuine apologies for hurting one another sprinkled in, our relationship eventually evolved into a comfortable family-like feeling. We were still there for each other but had our separate lives and no chemistry, just like healthy families should.

I began to notice there were still things about the way he lived that slightly bothered me, but now that he wasn't my husband, I would just walk away shaking my head instead of fighting and trying to get him to be different. I would often whisper to myself, "Thank goodness that is not my problem anymore."

However, when we were married, these same behaviors drove me insane. I would fight tooth and nail to get him to be different: to change and be a better person, be more like me. It struck me how strange it was that I stopped caring about these "flaws" once we were no longer together.

It is sad that most people don't accept others as they are in romantic relationships. The women I work with are guiltier of trying to get their partners to be different than the men I work with are. We as women are quite often trying to get our partners to change. We don't accept them and they feel that. When working with couples this is the dynamic I run into quite often: The woman needs the man to be or do something different and she pushes really hard to make it happen. The man ends up feeling unworthy, like he can never do anything right. It is quite sad.

My ex was a homebody. He would often sit in front of his computer screen from morning until night. I just couldn't understand how someone would want to stay in the house all the time and not go out and explore the world. When we were married, it felt like he was holding me back, and I took him staying in as a personal threat to my happiness, which was unfair of me to do. He was fine with it. It was his life, not mine.

One day after our divorce, I passed his bedroom to see him sitting on the bed in front of the computer as usual. It suddenly dawned on me that one of the reasons I couldn't accept this in him when we were married is because that behavior was *my* shadow self. Being numb to the world and not participating to the fullest is my biggest and worst fear.

My shadow self is unmotivated, lazy, uninspired and takes life for granted. I couldn't stand it in him because I couldn't stand the shadow side of myself. I had been born ready to explore this great big adventurous world. As a kid, my personal hell would be to be housebound. I would throw temper tantrums when I had to take a nap because I was sure that I was going to miss out on something fun and exciting while I was sleeping. Once I reached adulthood, I kept myself insanely busy to stave off a sense of deprivation. Back then, I still felt anxious if I was home with nothing to do. When it came to activity levels and our views on life, my ex and I were obviously a bad match from the start.

However, I realized that my disdain for his lifestyle was an indicator of my disdain for a deeper part of myself and my own fears. This realization gave me the opportunity to review all the things for which I had been so hard on him and to turn it around towards my own life.

I asked myself:

"Where am I not living life to the fullest?"
"What am I not accepting about myself?"
"What do I want to change for myself?"

Usually, the things that trigger us the most have something to do with our relationship with ourselves. Although I know that a partner who lacks the same motivation and lust for life that I have ultimately won't be a good fit for me, I did get to use it as a learning opportunity about my deeper fears. Even relationships that don't pan out, in the end, are there for a reason. I still suggest getting right with your love compass so you can pick a better match for yourself in the first place. And, if you always see everything that happens to you as something there to wake you up, you will never waste any of your precious time.

EXERCISE:
What is your shadow?

Go through past relationships and pick out the behaviors or habits that bugged you the most in your partner.

Ask yourself:

1. What does this resonate with in me?

   _____

   _____

   _____

   _____

   _____

2. What in my life do I need to change? Where am I afraid that I am not living my life like I want to?

   _____

   _____

   _____

   _____

   _____

Bunnies or chickens?

Back in 2000, my love life was a mess. I was heartbroken. I was picking terrible partners for myself and I wanted to get married and have children. I was in so much pain that I finally went to see Carl Buchheit, my amazing mentor and NLP teacher. I sat down in his cozy, familiar office with tears in my eyes as I shared my woes about my love life. I wanted him to fix it. I wanted him to fix my brain and unwire the destructive patterns that I kept finding myself in.

After the sad tale of the last break-up I had experienced, he calmly smiled at me and said, "Huh, you should have been married a bunch of times by now."

Confused, I asked, "What do you mean?"

"Well, you are bright, charming, and a beautiful woman. You should have been married and divorced a bunch of times by now." I sat with that for a minute.

"Well, I never seem to get that far," I explained.

After a moment's pause, he said, "It is like you are a bunny, hopping into the chicken coop to hang out with the chickens, all the time wondering why it is that you aren't mating." I laughed. But the meaning of this absurd scenario sunk in.

"So why are you hanging with the chickens and not the bunnies?" he asked me.

"Well, the bunnies are intimidating. If I hang out with them I might feel like a fraud. I mean, I am always doing better than the chickens so I don't feel nervous around them," I explained.

In that session, we uncovered some of my deep beliefs. I learned that my subconscious was telling me I wasn't as good as some of those men out there who had their lives together and could be great partners for me. And so, I was avoiding them, going for the men who needed help and weren't really living up to their potential because it felt safer. I knew I was valuable to them because I taught them things. They thought I was cool and smart and looked up to me. But I was deeply dissatisfied because I wasn't with my true equal. I wasn't with someone who would push me to grow or inspire me to live in my full potential. In a way, I was lucky I hadn't gotten married yet, not while I was hanging out in the chicken coop.

This talk of chickens vs. bunnies isn't meant to judge anyone or say that bunnies are better than chickens. We are all on our own paths. Chickens are on one path and bunnies are on another. It is just best if you mate within your own species.

I encourage you to do some self-exploration around this concept. Are you picking men who aren't challenging you, are living flaccid lives or are stuck and stagnate? If so, ask yourself, "What good thing comes from choosing those kinds of men?" Or, you can ask yourself, "What is the scariest thing about being with a man who has his life together and is living his purpose?" Your answers might be very revealing.

Your attitude while you are single affects your altitude

It is natural to desire love and a relationship. It is normal for your mind to drift to a possible future with a lover and dream about what life will be like and all the things you will do together. However, longing for love might make it take longer to find.

The mindset of longing often comes with a touch of pain or sadness. Often, melancholy thoughts sneak in because you don't yet have what you want in love. The desire for a partner might then become paired in your subconscious with thoughts of loneliness as you compare where you are versus where you want to be. It might start out feeling good to imagine how beautiful it will be when you meet your partner, but it won't be long before the brain will load up the pain that goes with not having this yet.

The subconscious always says YES!

The universe always mirrors back to you your own thoughts, words and feelings. You are the creator of your own destiny. With this comes responsibility for your own life.

If you really desire something, you need to make sure to be very specific and clear about what you want. Whatever it is you are broadcasting will get mirrored back to you.

Some people resonate more with an external source granting them their prayers or desires. Some people like to feel more in control of their own destinies and prefer to feel as if all that they want will come from them directly.

Whether it is God answering prayers, the universe co-creating with you or simply your own subconscious acting out your instructions, it doesn't matter WHY it works; it is important to know that whatever is at play, the thoughts and emotions that you cultivate are POWERFUL forces that will either answer your prayers or unknowingly sabotage your goals if you are not careful.

Words and emotions are so powerful that they become hypnotic suggestions to your subconscious. Because of this, it is very important that you are careful about HOW you are thinking about love and relationships. Your subconscious always says YES to you. Like a good, loyal soldier, whatever you directly or inadvertently say or think, you are sending messages of direction to your brain.

For example, if you are working with your compass and start to fantasize about your future love life and partner, you might say to yourself, "Ah that feels good. I really want that." The brain/god/universe says, "YES." Then if some sadness about not having it yet creeps in, you might say to yourself, "I might never find that. How sad; I might be alone forever." The brain/god/universe will say, "YES. You will be alone forever." And then it will go out and make that true as if you just gave it instructions. This is why it is so important to be very careful about what instructions you feed your brain. Longing usually comes with a touch of urgency and feeling desperate. Beneath the desperation is a belief that whatever it is you want won't come. This ends up being the message you are sending out:

"This might not come to me."

"YES, it won't come to you." The brain mirrors back.

What if you don't believe love is possible?

"The biggest obstacle is that I don't believe that love and relationships are possible, at least not how I want them to be. So how do I break out of my closed way of thinking even though I don't have any evidence that things can be different? Even if all I have for evidence is that love is painful and disappointing?" This is what Sue said to me the day she started the F.L.I.R.T. course.

It's tough when we've had no evidence that says that love will be the way we want it to be. Even worse, most of us have had strong evidence that it doesn't turn out the way we want it. But don't lose hope. There is a cure for a disappointed and disillusioned heart that projects all the disappointment from the past into the present and the future. Quite simply it is:

Faith

Faith is the concept of believing without proof. Faith is what you might have to hold onto while you read this book so that you can get the most out of what it has to offer. The principles in this book have the power to transform you and transform how your brain is seeing and handling relationships, but if you are already starting with a deficit, it will be hard for anything else to sink in. Your brain might kick out the things that will offer you the transformation you are seeking if you don't open up to the possibility even just a smidgen.

Give thanks for the parts that are trying to protect you

Negative Nelly and Doubting Debbie swooped in to protect you from heartbreak.

They vowed that they were never going to let you do anything ever again that will cause heartbreak and thank goodness for that. They are also the gatekeepers to your heart, and as they are blocking out potential heartbreak, they are also blocking out potential love, good people and positive experiences.

So how do we get those tough ladies to take a little break so you can maybe see the world, men and love a bit differently? How do we convince them that you will still be okay even if things don't turn out as planned? How do we convince them that getting your heart broken isn't as dangerous as it seems? Or, if you do happen to end up heartbroken somewhere along the way, how do we get them to understand that disappointment is a survivable feeling?

First things first. We employ some fail-safe features, some security measures so that you can open your heart but not be stupidly blind, letting things and people in that aren't good for you. You see, Nelly and Debbie came on the job because you had bad experiences in the past, either in past relationships or in your childhood. Whatever happened hurt so badly that Nelly and Debbie came running to the rescue to make sure THAT never happens again! And it won't. As long as you close your heart. As long as you harden and become bitter. As long as you sit behind your wall of distrust, condemning men and love and the stupid people who fall into their traps. Nothing will slip by, I promise. Your heart will be safe. But you will not be happy, nor will you get what you want in love.

So, let's have a conversation with Nelly and Debbie and ask them if, for the next few weeks while you read this book, they wouldn't mind going on a short vacation.

Faith will have to take their place. Faith that you won't get hurt. Faith that something else is possible. Faith that even if you do open up and get hurt that you will recover. Then when you are finished reading this book, if you think it is a good idea for them to be put back on the job, please invite them back. But if you can open your heart just a little bit, I promise, this book will be much more helpful.

Pessimism vs. Optimism

Six months after my divorce, I began to date casually. I use the term "date" loosely since it was basically just a series of first meetings with people who I had met online. I didn't have any second dates. I didn't find myself very interested in any of these people and was lukewarm at best about the concept of having another relationship in my life. I was angry about my past relationship mistakes, I was jaded and I was only dating because I thought that maybe if I met the right person, he would snap me out of the cynicism I was feeling. It was a strange place to find myself in because before I met my husband, I was positive about love. I was enthusiastic about meeting new people, and my dating life was much juicier as a result. Now I lacked commitment about finding a new partner. I was less than optimistic that love ever worked out anyway. My views on relationships were tinged with bitterness and hopelessness. You see, I had had a long career of troubled relationships, false hopes and broken hearts. After my short marriage ended, something in me had finally broken.

The hope that I'd hung onto in the past—the belief that I just hadn't met the right person yet—soon vanished and was replaced with a nagging feeling that all relationships always end in sorrow. If that was the case, why would I want to get into one again?

Logically, I knew that this wasn't the truth. But my brain only had evidence based on relationships that were a struggle or ended in disappointment, starting from my very first role model: My mom. Mom had her fair share of awful relationships, which is what my first experience of romantic love was based on. Unsurprisingly, I continued the pattern she had started.

There was nothing I could do to change my own mind about this because I didn't have any evidence to the contrary. Because my brain was lacking in positivity about love, I found myself indifferent when I would meet new people. I rolled my eyes at most men while swiping through online dating apps. I walked around in the world shut down, and my heart was essentially closed for business. There was no way I was going to meet Mr. Right or Mr. Prove Me Wrong About Love Guy. I was on a short path to a long life of being alone and bitter about it. I needed to find a different role model. I searched through my friends who were partnered up. Nope, I couldn't really land on one who I thought had a healthy, happy relationship.

I needed to look outside of what I knew. After talking to one of my friends about my failure to find evidence of happy love, she promised me that love was possible. Even though she herself had many heartbreaks in her past and was currently single, she was still optimistic. I had to find out how she kept her positivity even through loss and heartache. She told me she had many relatives who were in love, married and very happy. So even though she was having a slump, she knew it was still possible because she had proof. She saw them every holiday and every family gathering and grew up seeing them happy and staying in relationships and marriages that lasted through the years. She invited me over for Thanksgiving that year to witness the love these people shared with each other even after years of marriage. After observing the affection, respect and love that some of her sisters, cousins and aunties had, I felt a rekindling of my own hope. All I needed was some evidence that it was possible. If it is possible for one person, then it is possible for everyone!

EXERCISE:
Find a role model

Find a role model for the kind of relationship that you would like to have. You can search your friend group, family or even fictional characters if need be. The role model you select can serve as a guide for you on your path to love.

Notice what it is like to realize that healthy love is possible. I caution you not to look at happy relationships with jealousy. Instead, work on developing the mindset that if it is possible for them then it is more possible for you. The same is true when your friends and family find love or get married. Instead of envy or feeling sorry for yourself that you haven't found it yet, celebrate the fact that love is possible, which means there is more love in the world and more available for you.

2

Preparing for Healthy Love to Come In

We attract out there what is going on inside

Is clutter blocking your love life? Think of your life as a mirror of attraction. If your life feels chaotic or stressful, if you have things left undone or your environment is cluttered, if you are in dramatic situations constantly or if you are generally unhappy, it will either repel healthy men from wanting to get involved with you or it will attract someone whose life is also chaotic and a mess. Healthy, mature men are looking for an equal partner, not someone to save or fix. Most men of this caliber will be repelled by the drama that your life might be broadcasting.

Finding love is a holistic practice. It is about everything in your life lining up with your highest self so that you are a welcoming place for healthy love to come in. If you want a man who has his life together, then you need to have yours together. If you want a man who is good with his money, you need to be taking the same amount of care with your finances. Basically, if you want a man who is a good catch, you need to have your life together and also be a good catch.

If you are broken you might attract a fixer

Maybe you dream of finding your knight in shining armor. It might feel romantic for a man to swoop in to save you or take care of you. Back in the day, this was called a fairy tale romance. Today it is called codependent. I am not saying that it is wrong to take care of each other in a relationship. Healthy relationships do have an element of supporting one another and making sure the other person is all right. However, there is a big difference between supporting your partner and needing to fix him or his life. It is dysfunctional when the relationship is based on getting fixed or needing to fix someone. The danger of not having your life clear and cleaned up first is that you might attract a partner who likes and needs to fix women to feel good about himself. He might appear to be a knight in shining armor but what might be really going on under the surface is his own lack of self-worth. The problem with this scenario is that he will need you to stay "broken" in order to feel he is useful to you. If you do pull yourself together, you might become obsolete to him and he will leave. In addition, this is a terrible foundation to build a relationship on.

That said, if you already have your life together and a man does things here and there for you, it is a beautiful thing. The right man for you will want to make your life easier and to be of service. It becomes dysfunctional when you need him to help you all the time, you feel helpless without him or if he doesn't know any other way to connect with you if he's not saving you or doing something for you.

Karry came to me after her divorce. She had been married for ten years, and the biggest complaint in her marriage was that she felt lonely. Her husband Tom was quite often distracted and numbed out in front of the TV. Karry longed for connection and intimacy, but it quite often fell short. Except for when she was really depressed or emotionally falling apart. If she had a bad day at work or when her mom died or she was upset and sad about things, then her husband would pay attention and be really sweet and present with her. Over the years, she realized that she was leaning more and more into depression because she knew subconsciously that was the only way she got attention from him. It was similar to the scenario of a nurse who doesn't pay much attention to her children and can only relate to them when they are sick. The children compensate by coming down with reoccurring sickness frequently. The brain is a very powerful thing!

When women come to me wondering why they can't meet that special guy, we begin by looking at all aspects of their lives for clues to what might be blocking them. To prepare for healthy love to come in, you and your life need to be a strong, safe space for it to do so. A cluttered house, unfinished tasks, long to-do lists, old love tokens, ex-boyfriend clutter or even toxic people can be huge factors in a person's inability to attract the kind of partner who they want.

Before you are really ready for someone special to come into your life, you need to begin by making some space for this new person. And by that, I mean space in the physical environment, space in the mental environment and mostly space in your heart.

Sarah had a messy house and no love

When Sarah first walked into my office, she looked drained and tired. Her eyes lacked any emotion or sparkle, and her energy was dull. Sarah was thirty-seven years old at the time and all she craved in her life was to get married and have children. At thirty-seven, she felt time was running out. Her main complaint was that men never paid attention to her and she felt invisible to them. She hadn't even dated anyone in over seven years. She sat down in my office almost ready to give up. I explained to her that finding a healthy relationship is affected by many factors, and we set out to discover what was happening to keep her single. This is what we figured out: Sarah lived in a tiny studio in San Francisco, which is normal for that city. However, she had moved into her place two years prior and hadn't fully unpacked yet. There was a small pathway from her front door to her bed, and boxes were stacked up along every wall. She hated being at home. It felt dark and claustrophobic. She also told me about her job. She hated going to work. Her job was draining, and she really wanted to change careers into something she had always longed to do. Held back by fear, she stayed stuck in her current position instead. She was afraid to make the change and kept at it year after year. Because her apartment was so cluttered, she was often losing things and found herself unable to keep up with things that needed to be done. She made good money, but her finances also were so disorganized that she never had enough money accessible and was often late paying her bills. What I discovered about her social life was also a block to her finding a relationship. She had friends who were in the habit of dumping all of their problems on her, but when she needed support, they didn't really reciprocate. They tended to be negative and were always involved in some kind of drama. She didn't really enjoy hanging out with them but felt like she didn't have a choice because being with them was better than being alone.

When I asked Sarah why she stayed in these situations that were obviously making her unhappy and drained, this is what she told me: "When I find my partner, then my life will be different."

"Oh yes, the My Life Will Be So Much Better When I Have My Man Syndrome," I replied, with a smile because I see many women with this kind of thinking. Sarah explained to me that she hadn't unpacked her boxes because she figured when she met her guy that they would move in together. So why bother unpacking? She was too afraid to leave her career to pursue her dream but thought when she had a partner, she would feel braver. She rationalized this by explaining how he'd be there to bail her out in case she failed. Her money problems would go away because they would pool their resources, and she could also dump her negative friends because she would have him as a friend. The problem with this thinking is that because Sarah was stuck and her life was a mess, it was causing her to be invisible to men. She lacked radiance and joy. She looked expressionless and unapproachable. It was the very reason WHY she hadn't met someone yet. I told her lovingly, "Sarah, you need to make your life good now, or you will never meet a healthy partner." She hadn't realized she was relying on a man she hadn't even met yet to save her from her dissatisfaction. She was the one who needed to save herself.

The story has a happy ending though. When Sarah began to clean up the "clutter" that was blocking her radiance, her whole life changed, especially the way she felt about herself. It was fascinating to watch her transform before my very eyes over the course of the next couple of months. She was smiling more. There was a playful twinkle in her eye and she just glowed. Because she pulled her life together and decided to be happy now, she ended up meeting her future husband within that year.

How does cleaning your closet help you find your man?

Let's start with environmental clutter. Close your eyes and imagine an environment that you have been in the past where things are clean, organized and beautiful. Imagine it and remember how it felt to be there. Savor that feeling of being there in your body.

Now think of an environment where things were messy, dirty and disorganized and recall what it felt like to be there.

As you might have noticed, your environment affects how you FEEL, not just emotionally but also physically. It will either have you feeling relaxed, peaceful and clear, or it will make you feel stressed, unfocused, or icky.

People pick up on our internal state way more then we realize. Men are attracted to radiant, happy, relaxed, open women. If we don't have a clean, beautiful space to unwind in when we are home, we can't fully charge our radiant feminine essence.

Not to mention how it affects your energy when you are getting ready to go out into the world but you're unable to find things or there is clutter everywhere causing you stress.

If your home or other places where you spend time are cluttered or messy, it is taking more of a toll on you then you think. When you love your environment, that appreciation and love fills you up and helps you to de-stress.

EXERCISE:
Make your environment rejuvenating

1. Make a list of all the places that need to be cleaned out, or that are cluttered. These could be areas in your house like cupboards, closets, etc. Even if you can't SEE the clutter and it is hiding behind a closet door, it is still taking up unnecessary space in your life. This also includes other places where you spend time, like your desk at work or your car.

_____

_____

_____

_____

_____

2. After making your list of all the areas that need some attention, then make a schedule detailing how you want to begin to tackle it. Remember to make it doable. Set up little goals for yourself so it doesn't feel overwhelming. If you overwhelm your brain, it will quit before you even begin. It might be as simple as saying, "I am going to do clutter cleanup for only five minutes a day, or pick one area a week." If you really are feeling motivated, you can try to do it all at once. No matter which way you set it up, make sure you set yourself up to succeed and not to fail.

_____

_____

_____

_____

_____

What your brain sees will create emotional states

It is helpful to decorate your home to energetically feel like there is pairing or coupling energy. Your subconscious brain is very susceptible to the images it sees and it can begin to shape your beliefs about yourself and the world without you knowing it.

Shannon was lonely

Shannon was a creative person and a lover of art. She had been collecting paintings and photographs for fifteen years and was proud to display her collection in her small apartment. Shannon's main complaint in life and love was that she felt lonely and that was why she desperately wanted a life partner to ease the sense of aloneness. Her need often prompted her to pick men who weren't good for her because she just wanted somebody, anybody. She often settled, compromising her real desires. The relationships would eventually end in sorrow, which would then reinforce her loneliness.

Shannon's home and her mind were full of loneliness

Most of the works in Shannon's art collection depicted a solitary woman in a pensive or melancholy state. The common feelings that these paintings emanated were of loneliness. Although she resonated greatly with these images, and that is what attracted her to them on a subconscious level, having them surrounding her only perpetuated her feeling of sadness about being single. She lived in a very small apartment and didn't have room for many things. She had impeccable taste and prided herself on being a minimalist. To save space, she had a single bed and only one cup, one dish and one bowl. Energetically, she wasn't even equipped to invite anyone into her world because there was nothing there for them. What all of this

*ended up saying to her subconscious was that no one was welcome in her home.
When she realized that her surroundings were reinforcing her feelings of loneliness,
she made the big decision to sell her beloved paintings. She then began to collect
art that held feelings of connectedness and intimacy. This reminded her of the love
she wanted to feel and made her happy when looking at them. She arranged her
furniture to fit a double bed and bought a set of two place settings.*

*After her home transformation, she reported: "Coming home now feels pleasur-
able as it gives me a glimpse of what it will feel like when I have a man in my life.
It used to feel so bleak and lonely in my home, which really affected my energy level
in and outside of my home."*

Now take a look at your own environment and see how you feel in it. Ask
yourself if it is a good place for love to come in.

Mental clutter makes you invisible to men

To-do lists. We all have them. The bad news is they will never go away.
Part of life is having to take care of things, pay bills, grocery shop, pay taxes,
clean the house, plan social events, go to work, etc. The number of things we
need to take care of can sometimes be overwhelming.

Have you ever been driving or walking down the street while at the same
time going through your mental list of what you have to do that day? Or when
you are out and about shopping or grabbing lunch, is your brain occupied
with the tasks on your running to do list? Have you ever had this thought
circling around in your mind, "Don't forget to…don't forget to…?"

Most people have difficulty being present and focused. Our brains are
naturally wired to be active and "think" about things. As annoying as it can be,
your brain is actually trying to take care of you by playing the tasks and lists
over and over lest you forget.

The problem with that, though, is that it takes you away from your present. It takes you away from connecting with people and it makes you invisible to men. Women always complain to me that they don't know where to find good men to date. I smile every time I hear this. "Look around," I usually tell them. "You are around good men all the time." There doesn't have to be a separation between "looking for my partner" time and everyday life. You can meet your potential partner at the grocery store, the bank, walking down the street, in a coffee shop, ANYWHERE.

Unfortunately, we are often caught up in our own thoughts and to-do lists when we are out in the world, blocking us from really connecting with anyone. Maybe we miss the cute guy in the grocery store checking us out. Or you might miss opportunities to catch someone's eye and smile, letting him know you are open for connection. It really is sad.

Close the brain loop

Like I mentioned, your brain is designed to keep looping until a task is finished and checked off the list. It is trying to help you out. There are ways to help the brain relax and trust that things will be taken care of so it can shut up and stay focused on the present. Some simple things you can do include: first write down all the things that need to be done and make sure you check them off to give your brain some satisfaction of completion. Next is my secret, surefire way to get the brain to calm the heck down. Write down on a calendar either when you will have the task finished or when you will need to start it. Remember what your brain sees on a daily basis will send out signals in your subconscious to match and create. So even glancing at a calendar and seeing a task completed on a certain date will set in motion your brain completing it. Also, when you write a task down, your brain won't feel the need to keep reminding you to get it done. I recommend writing these things on a paper calendar in a book or hanging it on the wall. Use whatever you might glance at often. See how your energy changes when you can relax, knowing that you have your life handled.

Toxic people suck....your soul

Motivational speaker. Jim Rohn said, "You are the average of the five people you spend the most time with." I heard this at a conference I attended one year. It struck me deeply because, at the time, I was trying to build my career and find my life partner, and both of these tasks seemed challenging if not impossible. I realized that I had a people clutter problem.

I consider myself a loyal person, and I had a group of friends that I was spending time with out of obligation. We had been friends for twenty years but we had grown in different directions. I was trying to make my life better. I had big plans and dreams, but they were stuck and had been for a long time. These friends, on the other hand, weren't interested in making their lives better or in growing, and some of them were even being self-destructive with their habits and lifestyle choices. They often complained and were quite negative as well. I didn't really get much out of being around them, but I felt obligated to see them since we had been friends for such a long time.

I was trying to find a healthy love partner while trying to launch my career and business. If what Jim Rohn said was true—if I was the average of these friends—then I knew I needed to change some things or I was going to stay as stuck as they were.

I wasn't judging them. It just became clear that these people were on a different path than I was, and that we had grown apart. People come in and out of our lives all the time and it is okay to let them go when the time comes. I knew deep down that they weren't feeding my growth. I would often feel drained and tired after spending time with them. They were stuck in the same loop of partying and shallow conversation. I decided I was going to stop giving them so much of my time. Guess what? The relationships just naturally faded. It became apparent that I was the one holding on and they didn't contribute much to our staying close.

Space opened up for me to spend time with people who were on a path similar to mine. Being around positive people gave me such a boost in motivation that my business took off, and my dating life changed drastically once I was more positive.

Your brain is like a sponge. It is constantly absorbing energy. Negative people suck your energy and leave you feeling depleted. We will talk more about radiance and attraction later, but yes, it will suck your own positivity.

Men are natural drama avoiders. A man will want to be there for the woman in his life, but if she appears to have too many dramatic interactions with people or if she has dramatic, toxic friends around her, he will naturally want to run. Who your friends are says a lot about who you are. This man will also be trying to figure out if the woman he's dating will be a good fit for him, and if he senses drama—even if it isn't hers—he won't want to be her forever guy.

Another thing that keeps women giving their energy to toxic people is an unworthy belief structure. People who don't have high self-esteem will often put up with bad behavior from others because they don't feel like they deserve better. They fear they won't have other people in their lives if they walk away from the toxic ones. We will talk more about how your beliefs create all of your experiences in the next chapter.

Roommates from Hades

Janice lived with a much older roommate in a beautiful apartment in the Mission District of San Francisco. She had found the place on Craigslist after a six-month search for a place to live. When she met Michael, he was sweet enough and he kept to himself. It felt like a perfect living situation for Janice. Yvonne, who had placed the ad, was his former roommate. She was moving out and needed to find someone to replace her. That someone was Janice. After about a month, Janice began to realize that this former roommate was actually Michael's much younger ex-girlfriend. They had broken up, but the woman was still his main caretaker because he was sick with COPD and essentially dying. Yvonne never moved her stuff out of the apartment, and she would let herself in and out all day.

It felt weird, but Janice didn't say anything. That is, she didn't say anything until Yvonne started going into Janice's room and dictating what time Janice could come in at night so she didn't wake Michael.

Yvonne was very controlling and territorial over her former home and it made Janice feel like an unwelcome guest. What's more, Michael was secretly smoking cigarettes even though he already had a lung condition because of his 50-year habit. He'd had a hard life and it was apparent that he wanted to die. He had already given up.

At the time, Janice was seriously seeking to find her life partner, but her living situation was taking a toll on her search. Being around someone who had given up on life and was self-destructing, not to mention the constant upset by the former roommate trying to manipulate the household, caused Janice to feel drained, tired and unable to relax in her own home. She rarely had the energy to go and meet new people, and she didn't feel comfortable having people over to her house. When she realized that this toxic situation might be one of the reasons she was still single, she set out to find her own place right away. Finding a place to live in San Francisco is no small feat, but she knew she had to make a change. With focus and tenacity, she moved into her own studio apartment. Now her home feels like a sanctuary, as it should. She can relax and enjoy her time there. She feels comfortable inviting people over. All of this shifted her energy immediately, including her dating energy.

How to know when someone is toxic

You will know when people are toxic by how you feel around them and how you feel after spending time with them. You will know if someone is toxic if you feel drained, stressed, de-energized, agitated or upset. That doesn't mean that your friends can't have a bad day now and then. What I am talking about is a consistent sense of a lower vibration.

Here are some clues to tell if the people in your life are toxic:

They are usually negative about things.
They complain a lot.
They act like victims.
They are controlling.
They talk about themselves without asking about you.
They redirect conversations to be about them or what they want to talk about.
They have self-destructive habits.
They are manipulative.
They are condescending and rude.
You don't have fun around them.

If you are starting to realize you might have some of these kinds of people in your life, I suggest making a plan to either remove them or figure out a way to minimize contact. Sometimes family members can be toxic. I am not a fan of disowning family if you can avoid it, but you might want to brainstorm ways in which you can make the contact less toxic for you. You might need to have stronger boundaries or a conversation with someone or to not spend as much time around them.

Bosses and co-workers are also difficult situations to walk away from. You could quit your job, but this isn't always possible. People spend most of their time at work, so if you are getting drained by the relationships at your job you will have little radiant energy left over for your love life. I strongly recommend thinking of ways to clean up negative energy at work or consider finding a job that feels better.

Positive people

Positive people are like vegetables. You can never have too many of them. These people in your life will leave you feeling positive, full of energy, inspired, understood and loved. If you have more of them in your life, just think how it might affect you. When you surround yourself with this kind of energy you will be happier, lighter and more joyful. All very good qualities for attraction.

Pam was searching for her partner when she learned about toxic people blocks. At the time, she had a few close girlfriends who were constantly complaining about upsets or people in their lives. The biggest things they complained about were men and how hard dating was. Every time Pam got together with them it was always the same story. So-and-so did A, B and C and that means he must be an S.O.B. And so on. Pam also became aware that her friends used her as a sounding board and a dumping place for their negativity. However, they were rarely available for her when she needed them or was having a problem with something. This imbalance was a sure sign of a toxic relationship. She also realized that being around the constant complaining about men and dating had sunk into her own subconscious, and she wasn't feeling that open to men and dating anymore either. She had begun to believe that men were users and scumbags because of her girlfriends' points of view. This is not a great mindset when it comes to looking for a partner.

Once she realized this, she had a conversation with one of her friends and explained that, while she loved her and wanted to be there for her, her negative viewpoints were bringing her down. Luckily, her friend hadn't realized the effect she was having on Pam and was thankful for the insight. In fact, her complaining was dropping her own energy and she was happy to try something else. They made a pact to speak positively about men and dating, and, even if there were issues, to always look for the good in any situation. The time they spent together became more uplifting. Pam began to enjoy her time with her friend and they encouraged each other to stay open and positive.

If you really do value keeping someone in your life, then I recommend having a conversation with them about whatever feels draining to you so you might be able to resolve it without having to throw away the relationship. If, after an honest, loving conversation, the relationship can't be fixed, at least you know you tried before walking away or distancing yourself.

Your ex might be blocking you from finding new love

As I mentioned before, the people in your life will affect you greatly. Past lovers will also leave a lasting impression in your psyche and can sometimes block new love from coming in. Even if it feels like you are over your ex, the blocks can be sneaky and not that obvious.

Maybe you are still angry or resentful at how things ended. Maybe you are still sad and missing him. Maybe you are hoping he will come back or maybe you feel like you will never meet anyone else like him.

If his energy is still hanging out in your sphere even just a little bit, then he is blocking you from finding someone else.

It might be time to clean up your ex clutter!

Memorabilia:

As you are doing your environmental clutter cleanup, pay some special attention to items in your space that remind you of your ex, such as gifts that he gave you, photos, or even clothes that you might have worn on your special dates with him. Remember that the things that your subconscious brain sees will get you to feel certain emotions associated with the objects. Pay attention to which emotions these objects from past loves bring up in you.

The one who got away

When I set out to clean up my life to find love, I found a love letter tucked away in a box written by a man who I had deemed, "The one who got away." When I read the 17-year-old letter, I was immediately overtaken with emotion and tears. Surprised at my emotional reaction, I realized I had been hanging on to that letter because I wanted to remind myself that someone really good did love me once. But alongside the positive message was regret and deep sadness because I had pushed him away. I was so wounded back then, and couldn't handle a good guy really adoring me. From that point on I had made him into my ideal partner and felt that no one would ever live up to him. Guess what? It was true. For seventeen years, I had been comparing every man I had dated to him and they had never matched up. I knew I needed to burn that letter. I had been holding onto him and the ideal I had created. It was one of the reasons I was still single and kept pushing good guys away —because they weren't him. It was so hard to burn that letter, but once I did I felt an incredible lightness and space open up inside me. I silently thanked him for showing me love. I started thinking there would be someone else out there for me. If I found it once, I can find it again. It was extremely freeing not having him still in my heart as the one who got away.

If you look at an item associated with your ex and you feel upset or sad or you begin to miss him, it is time to get rid of it or at least put it in a box deep in your closet. If you can't get rid of it, then ask yourself, "How is it serving me to hold on to it?" Living with ghosts will do nothing for your future love life. You might have to be brave and get rid of something even if you don't want to. The simple act of doing so makes a statement to your subconscious that you deserve happiness, you are making space for it and you trust that something good will come in and replace what you just let go of. If you look at a piece of memorabilia left behind and you feel neutral about it or even feel content, without longing for that person or relationship, then it is probably safe to keep around.

Anger and sadness keep you stuck to your ex

After a breakup, no matter how mutual the decision was, how long the relationship or whether you left or he left, it is normal to go through the grief of loss. You will naturally feel angry, sad and lonely, and go over the events leading to the breakup over and over in your mind. All this is completely normal. Eventually, though, your heart will heal. It will get less and less painful and not occupy your every waking moment.

It is good to give yourself time to heal before you move on and date. To really give yourself permission and time to properly grieve is a very loving thing to do for yourself. It is also normal to just want to push the fast-forward button and pass over the pain and try not to feel it. I hate to tell you this, but there is no way to avoid the pain of the loss. The fastest way through it is to dive into it. Eventually, you will get to the acceptance stage, even if you feel like you never will. Just know this: how you feel will always change. Always.

At times, though, there are hidden scars left over from breakups, even if it feels like you "are so over him." It is good to find out if any hidden snags might be keeping you stuck.

EXERCISE:
Emotional cleanup

Think back through your dating and relationship life. Are there any exes who you might still feel angry, resentful or sad about? You will be able to tell if anything is still lurking if you make a picture of them in your mind and really pay attention to the way you feel about them. Think about if there is anything you want to say to them. If you feel anything but friendly neutrality, it might be worth a little exploration to find out what still needs to be healed.

If you feel anger or sadness, what is it specifically you are sad or angry about?

_____

_____

_____

_____

_____

Is there anything good that came out of the relationship?

_____

_____

_____

_____

What was the most valuable thing you learned?

_____

_____

_____

_____

What good thing comes to you by hanging on to sadness or anger?

_____

_____

_____

_____

_____

Sometimes we get stuck, hanging onto those emotions because it feels like if we stop being sad or angry then we will be completely done with the relationship. Yes, it is true. If you still feel an emotional charge around someone then you ARE still in a relationship with him even if he isn't physically there. If you are still in a relationship energetically with your ex then you are technically not single, and this will block your next partner from coming in.

What can you do to let it, and him, go? What can you acknowledge about him that will help you forgive and/or walk away with confidence? What was your part in the breakdown of things? Can you look at the situation as a learning experience? You both taught each other something and that is the absolute truth. Even if you will never truly know what you taught him, rest assured that you do have an impact on people. Everyone has an impact on people they are with, especially when they are intimate with each other.

I thought I had healed my past

I had been dancing around the subject of my bitterness and closed heart even a year and a half after my divorce. I could sense the tightness in my chest whenever I thought of being in another relationship. I felt angry, hardened and very hopeless that any relationship would ever be different from the many past disappointments that I had already experienced.

I had been half-heartedly dating and got half-hearted men and experiences to come my way, making my hopelessness justified. Still, deep down in there was a glimmer that MAYBE I could have something different, something that was magical and satisfying, an inspiring love that didn't bait and switch on me.

Even though I knew my bitterness was one of the biggest blocks to finding this relationship I really did long for, I couldn't seem to shake the feeling of hardness in my body and energy. No amount of willing it away could shake it loose.

At a meditation retreat, I decided that the focus of my retreat would be to heal my heart and see if I could open it up to love again. Deep into the meditation practice, I fell into a vortex that sucked me into what felt like a tunnel. It was a hall, so to speak, where all my past heartbreaks lived. It seemed like a museum to pain, loss and disappointment. I passed by all of my past loves in reverse order, starting with my recent ex-husband, and landed all the way back standing in front of my father. The emotional abuse that I had suffered at his hand and the impact that it had on all my relationships that followed became so viscerally clear. The realization of this overwhelmed my body with its gravity and physical pain in my heart. I began to weep uncontrollably. It was as if forty-seven years of tears finally gave way. When it subsided I felt cleaned out, free and open. When I came out of the meditation vision, the bitterness was gone. I had let my grief break my heart open. The bitterness I had been experiencing had been with me since I was a child and the walls had grown thicker and thicker with each failed attempt at love and connection.

I had held on to the hardness as a way to be strong. The abuse that I had been through would have crushed me as a young one if I hadn't been hardened to it. But that same hardness that pulled me through my childhood was backfiring now in romantic love. I had been entering most relationships with an awareness that someone could hurt me and probably would at any given moment. The only question was *when* they would disappoint me, abandon me or suffocate me as my mentally ill father did.

Because I was waiting for it to happen, guess what always happened? Some form of abandonment, un-trustworthy action or using me for their gain. The first step to unlocking this cycle was to finally let myself feel the pain, let myself break down and be vulnerable about it. Once I did that, it was as if the cycle finally had a chance to complete. These unfinished chapters were hanging out both in time and in the space of my heart still, like an open case waiting for resolve. The resolve was to feel that which I could not have possibly felt when I was going through it.

EXERCISE:
Healing Your Heart

1. What heartbreak are you still holding on to that is clouding your possible next chapter or relationship?

_____

_____

_____

_____

_____

What do you need to feel or acknowledge to finally let it be over?

_____

_____

_____

_____

_____

Victim or victor?

Sometimes we hold onto grudges and feelings of being a victim which will keep you stuck in a never-ending loop.

After my divorce, I was stuck in a negative thought cycle of feeling like I had lost and my ex-husband had won. I lost everything and he gained everything by being with me. You see, I moved out of my rent-controlled apartment in San Francisco so we could have a bigger (and more expensive) space together. I helped him start his business. He got to easily follow in my footsteps on the path that I worked years to carve out. I supported him while he grew his business. I pushed him to be a better man and partner. We struggled. He did the work but things changed too slowly to save our marriage and it all fell apart. He continued to do the emotional work on himself that I had pushed him into even after we split up. When he was ready for a new relationship, I felt like he had grown so much and I was resentful. I didn't want to be the one who got him ready for his next relationship when all I got was the hard part. Not to mention that our relationship felt like the last straw in a long string of failed loves. It felt like this one had finally broken me and my spirit. I was playing the victim. The longer I held onto the injustice of this situation, the worse I felt and the more stuck I became. It wasn't until I was crying my eyes out, convinced that he had ruined love for me forever, that his next partner should send me a thank-you card for all the shit I put up with and feeling so sorry for myself, when the words, "every devil is an angel in disguise," bubbled up in my thoughts.

It struck me that even though I was villainizing my ex-husband, in fact, he had taught me a lot about boundaries in relationships. I learned about over-giving and the ways that I had shut down instead of communicating openly. This is something I learned how to master with him simply because I had no choice. Not having good boundaries in my love life had always been a problem for me, and with him, I had finally had a partner who I really needed to have them with as he was good at crossing them.

He could have been seen as a devil, but the lessons he taught me actually made him an angel that helped point me in the right direction on my soul's journey. For that, I could be thankful and stop being a victim. It was important for me to notice that I chose him. I chose to stay in the relationship even though there were red flags. I chose to give everything I gave. Instead of beating myself up about my choices (which I was also good at doing), I realized that my soul/subconscious chose this so that I could transform. Then I became a victor instead of a victim.

When you are in victim mode it takes a lot of energy to hold on to all the wrongs that have been done to you. Once you release all the past hurts and move forward, you can truly be free. You will not have any space for new love to come in if you are a victim or if you're holding onto past hurts or wrongs. It is imperative that you let it all go now.

Don't generalize

One reason your brain can get you stuck around love is that it is designed to be an incredibly efficient learning machine. Its main job is to learn. So, when you have negative experiences in love and relationships, your brilliant brain can also make the mistake of generalizing what it learned in your past. For instance, if you had a boyfriend who cheated on you or was abusive or self-centered, quite often your brain will begin to create beliefs about men in general. Men are cheaters. Men are selfish. Men are dangerous. It does this because it is trying to keep you safe, but those generalized beliefs will also keep you single, alone and miserable. We will talk more about beliefs later. For now, just notice if your past relationships are coloring what you think might happen in your future relationships. If so, it would be helpful to realize that there are many different types of men and love experiences out there, and just because it was one way in the past it doesn't have to be the same moving forward.

3

You Get What You Believe
or
Your Brain Might Be Ruining Your Love Life

You get what you believe

What you believe will always filter what you are able to experience. Beliefs dictate what you call into your life. What you believe about men, love and relationships might block you from picking good partners, and your beliefs about yourself will color how you feel about **everything**. Not only do they shape how we feel but our beliefs also control our behavior.

What we believe about some things are obvious. We have political beliefs. We have beliefs about how people should treat each other. We even might have religious and spiritual beliefs that shape our choices. However, some of our deeper beliefs about ourselves or life, and even beliefs about love and relationships are often hidden. Even though you might not be aware of them, they will still act as a filter on how you see reality. For example, if a person has the belief that men are selfish, then most likely what her brain will filter out and delete are all the men who are NOT selfish because it will pick up on all the acts that men do that could be interpreted as selfish. Our brain likes to match what we see "out there" with what we believe, and it filters out the rest.

Your beliefs are like tinted sunglasses

Your beliefs will color your world and your experiences in the same way that your perception will be altered if you put on colored sunglasses. Imagine putting on blue-tinted sunglasses and looking out at the world. Everything is still there but now it all has a blue tint to it. Now imagine putting on the "glasses" of "I'm not attractive" and look out at the world. You will see everything with a tint of that belief. It will color your experiences and most likely will change how you think and behave as well.

Reality is not real

Our powerful, wonderful brains are designed to learn. They are efficient and amazing. However, the ways they are designed to be skillful learners are the same ways they can get us very stuck in certain places. In order for your brain to learn and be efficient, it uses particular learning strategies: generalization, deletion and distortion. These strategies actually change a person's reality so that he or she can function better.

The brain generalizes information

You can walk into any room, even a room you have never been in before, and you will most likely know how to turn the lights on. That is because long ago, you learned how to turn on a light switch and your brain generalized that learning to all light switches. This is a very important function for learning. If you have already learned how to drive, most likely you will be able to drive any car you get into, even if it is unfamiliar. The way that our brain generalizes learning makes our lives very productive. As toddlers, we learned a lot about how to navigate in the world. We learned how to walk, talk, open things, close things, about the laws of gravity and much more. One big achievement for little ones (and a nightmare for parents) is when they learn how to open doors. Imagine what it would be like as an adult to have to relearn how to open every unfamiliar door that you came across, as if you were a toddler again. It would take forever to get in and out of every room and building that you entered. So yes, to be able to generalize what our brain learns is a really good thing for us. However, it is also one of the things that can get us stuck, especially in love and relationships.

Along the path of love and dating, we all hit some bumps in the road. We often run into common themes of rejection, heartbreak, betrayal, longing, not being treated how we want to be treated or not finding the right partner for us. When we experience pain in our relationships, we take those experiences and put them in the file folders in our brains labeled "relationships: what to watch out for." And then the next time we find ourselves beginning to date someone, our brilliant, helpful brains will take out the file folders to make sure we don't make the same mistakes that we made last time. "Avoid these situations that will make you feel bad!" it says. Our brains learn very quickly when pain is involved, whether it is emotional or physical pain. For example, many curious one-year-olds on their first birthdays will attempt to stick their fingers into the flames of their birthday candles if their parents aren't keeping a close eye on them. If they burn their fingers, chances are that will be the last time they stick their fingers into candles. This learning is a good thing. It keeps us safe, but, it also doesn't allow us to see specific incidents clearly. It can make us approach future relationships with a preconceived idea of what relationships feel like, what men are like and what we should or should not do to avoid pain, all based on past learning. The problem with that is we might project negative images on people, based on the past, without really seeing them clearly for who they are. We might also interpret their words or behaviors wrongly based on "lessons" we learned from the past. It is really good to learn from our past mistakes, but it is also helpful to keep from jumping to conclusions and assumptions and to actually get the information you need in order to make decisions about that particular person and that unique situation. Everyone is different and every situation is different. It is good to be aware of potential problems but also to keep an open mind to be sure.

How generalization keeps us stuck and limited

Jackie, one of the F.L.I.R.T. Course participants, came to me with such a dilemma. She had just recently met this amazing man but was so worried that he was cheating on her. She was constantly on edge and checking up on him in various ways. If he didn't call her three times a day, her brain instantly went down the path that he was cheating. If he didn't pay complete attention to her all the time, he must be cheating and there must be another woman. When I was coaching her through some of this worry and the fights that were happening between her and her new boyfriend, she told me that all of her boyfriends had cheated on her in the past. But what was more interesting is that when we dug deeper, what I really found out is that not ALL of them really cheated, but only one of them actually did that she had proof of. However, her brain took the pain of that betrayal and instructed her to always watch out for it so that she would never be caught off-guard and be made a fool of again. When boyfriends after the cheater came along and behaved in ways that seemed "suspicious," her brain got the confirmation it was looking for, "Yes, they must be cheating." Even if she didn't have concrete proof, it must be so. These were signs she had missed with her cheating boyfriend that her brain was determined to never miss again.

This might sound like a good plan in theory, but the reality of this set-up was that every man who later came into her life was immediately under suspicion. She had generalized a learning/belief that all men cheat and you cannot trust them.

Unfortunately, her new boyfriend was under attack for something he would never do, and it was about to drive him away. Luckily, after going through the course and working on unwiring this generalization, she was able to look at the real man in front of her and stop looking at him as a generalization. She began to see that his specific behavior and personality was not at all like the man who had betrayed her so many years before, and that being a cheater wasn't inherent in ALL men, but only in specific men with certain values and morals or a lack thereof.

Things we learn in our early years become the most stuck

The things that we learn in childhood get anchored deeper into our psyche than the things we learn as adults. As children, we are learning more, as well as faster, than we will as adults. This is mostly because we have much more to learn and our survival depends on it. As children, our brains are constantly trying to figure out the "rules" of life and how we are supposed to navigate it so we can get it right and not die. Unfortunately, we are often making big decisions about life and ourselves based on a little child's limited view and experience that will get set as true. Then as adults, we are still living with a child's perspective and beliefs of the world. It would be really great if some of these deeper beliefs changed with time, like the belief in Santa Claus or the Easter Bunny, for instance. There was a point in your life that you stopped believing it because it wasn't true and it didn't make sense anymore. Unfortunately, we don't seem to outgrow deeper beliefs unless we manually go in and get them updated.

I think of it as outdated software. Your brain is running certain software that dictates what you see, do and believe. This software hasn't been updated, and most of the time you are running outdated versions of how you see life and yourself based on a much younger you. In fact, as adults, we are usually still trying to survive our childhoods, because that part of your brain doesn't update on its own and doesn't understand growing up and time passing.

Let's visit Jackie again

When I worked with Jackie to figure out why she was unable to trust men, what we uncovered wasn't just that her boyfriend had cheated on her in the past. As it turned out, what was actually more impactful were her experiences with her father when she was young, which left her feeling unable to trust him. He had a very bad temper and would explode quite often without warning. Her little brain made very accurate calculations of how to survive that situation. With a father whose anger was unpredictable, her "system" came up with a very good plan to not trust him at all so she wouldn't be caught off guard. As long as she assumed he would blow up at any moment, she could predict it and be safe. Later in life, she applied that lesson to all men. As long as she never trusted them, she would be safe. When her ex-boyfriend actually did do something to break her trust, her brain grabbed on to that incident as more evidence to prove her theory. "See! I told you men were not trustworthy!" It was safer for her to suspect even the trustworthy ones. It had been set up in her brain that trusting was the most unsafe thing she could do. Luckily, with some belief re-patterning, her brain finally got the update it needed and she saved her relationship with her new boyfriend as she began to trust him more and more.

The brain deletes information so we don't get overwhelmed

Although the brain is an incredibly complex organ, it's not able to process the billions of bits of information that flood it every second. There are filters in your brain that protect it from becoming overwhelmed with too much input. These filters control how much information can come in. Approximately only 2,000 bits of information per second enter the brain. To do this filtering, the brain will pick up on things that it already knows, recognizes and understands first. The rest of the information gets deleted unless the brain is in the process of conscious learning (for example, going to a class to learn something new). The brain loves to match patterns. If we already have experience with a certain something, when faced with a repeat experience, the brain will look for what it already knows. If we have an established belief about something, it will pick up on the things it sees that match that belief and then delete everything else that doesn't match up.

Let's take, for instance, a woman who has had the experience in the past that men are insensitive and selfish. Her brain will make a file folder called "selfish, insensitive men." Because she already has an experience of that, her brain will pick up on all the insensitive selfish behavior in men that she sees all around her. She will see it on TV, she will see it on the street and she will pay attention to it when her girlfriends are complaining about their love lives. She will see it in the men she dates and tries to form relationships with. Every time she sees or hears of selfish, insensitive behavior in men, her brain will grab on to it and put it into the already known folder in her brain. With more evidence, that belief gets stronger and stronger. She might be "deleting" all the men (and behavior) all around her that are kind, thoughtful and chivalrous. There is nowhere to put this information, and nothing her brain can do with this information because it doesn't match up to what she already believes or has experienced. As such, it gets thrown out.

This deletion process is helpful to keep our system from becoming over-loaded, but it also is a good way of having a lopsided view of the world and experiences.

When Karen came to the F.L.I.R.T. program she was depressed and feeling hopeless. She felt that joining the program was her only hope and last chance to get love right. In her experience, men didn't notice her. She felt invisible. She felt worthless. She reported that when she went out, all of her girlfriends would get hit on and that men paid attention to them but never her. It hurt so much that she finally just stopped going out altogether. As we dove deeply into her belief structure, I discovered some more information. Additionally, her brain had been deleting the fact that there were some men who paid attention to her when she was out and about. Not only that but there was a man she worked with who she said always flirted with her. When I asked her why she didn't go for it, she simply replied that if he was interested in her then there must be something wrong with him.

Just sit with Karen's statement for a minute. What does that tell you about what she must believe about herself? "If someone is interested in her then there must be something wrong with him!" Karen had some pretty massive insecurities, and deep down didn't feel like she was good enough. So, when she was out with her girlfriends, she secretly compared herself to them when men would talk to them. Her brain would file away evidence in her folders "of not good enough." Another tricky thing her brain did was actually deleting the men who were talking to her and interested in her because it didn't make sense to her belief system.

You will know when someone is deleting and generalizing information when they say things like "**all** men, **every** relationship, men **never** talk to me…" Those words *all, never, always* are a sure sign that some information is being deleted.

Distortion and the brain's creativity

Distortion is another of the brain's creative ways to deal with information.

The brain doesn't like to be proven wrong. It is like a good prosecuting attorney, and it will only gather evidence based on what it is trying to prove. Sometimes it will distort information so that it will fit into what we already believe.

Information is just neutral. It is what we make it mean that creates our reality. The brain is a meaning-making machine. It makes everything represent or stand for something. The question is: Is it creating meanings that hurt or help you get what you want?

Jessica had a strong, deep belief that men would always abandon her. It sat right on top of a deep identity belief that she wasn't lovable. When she began dating Tom, she was on edge most of the time. Every time he didn't call or make plans with her or he went out with his friends, she was sure that he wasn't interested in her anymore. She would panic and get more and more insecure. Tom was living his life and having a healthy separation between his life and their shared life, but Jessica needed constant reassurance. She would often call him up out of the blue to ask him if he was breaking up with her. He would assure her that he wasn't but it never eased her mind.

One night after Tom had told her his guy friends were coming over for a guy's poker night, Jessica's fear hit a fever pitch. She was sure they were inviting other women over and possibly strippers. Her fear was driving her mad, so she went over to his house at 10 PM in the hopes of catching him in the act. Convinced she would find scantily clad women dancing around for the men, and one most likely sitting on Tom's lap, she burst through the front door to see five guys sitting around a table playing cards. No women. Tom was appalled by Jessica's behavior and lack of trust in him, and he ended up breaking up with her. Jessica's brain distorted the reasons why he broke it off and grabbed onto the breakup as a rejection and abandonment by yet another man. She created her worst fear, unable to see that it was her insecurity that drove her to behave in such a way that she essentially drove Tom away.

EXERCISE:
What is your brain doing?

1. What might you be deleting, distorting or generalizing that is coloring your story of men, love and relationships?

_____
_____
_____
_____
_____

2. What are some of the all, never or always words you might be using or saying to yourself?

_____
_____
_____
_____
_____

Is your past is getting in the way of your future?

We will be paying a lot of attention to our beliefs throughout this book. The sad truth is this: if you don't shift your limiting beliefs about yourself, love, men or what is possible for you, then NOTHING in your life will shift. You will never be able to have the kind of love life that you want if you don't take a look at these underlying beliefs and do something to change what they are saying to you.

Have you ever felt like it doesn't seem to matter how many self-help books you read, workshops you go to or online dating hours you put in, you just feel like **nothing** is changing? If you have limiting beliefs about who you are and what you deserve or negative views about men or painful stories you tell yourself about love and relationships then, unfortunately, you will continue to be stuck in the same painful situations that you have had over and over again.

Belief Cycle:

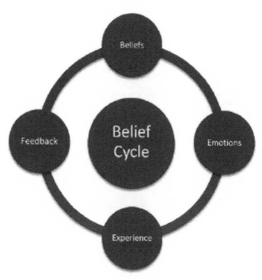

What we believe will cause us to feel a certain way. These emotions will cause us to behave according to how we feel. Not only that, but because of distortion, generalization and deletion, we can only have experiences that match up to what we already believe. Every time we have a matching experience, it becomes more evidence and turns into a feedback loop making the belief stronger.

EXERCISE:
Your story about love

1. Make a list of your limiting beliefs about men, relationships and love.

_____

_____

_____

_____

_____

2. On a scale of 1 to 10, how possible do you feel it is to get what you want as far as love and relationships go?

_____

_____

_____

_____

_____

3. How do you feel these beliefs are helping you? Yes, I did say helping you, because everything our brain is doing or not doing is for a very good reason, even if it is a hidden one.

_____

_____

_____

_____

_____

4. How are these beliefs blocking you?

_____

_____

_____

_____

_____

Repeating patterns and finding the hidden beliefs

Hidden beliefs and blocks can be like icebergs. Maybe you can only see the very surface of it but the vast majority of the glacier is hidden. These hidden, limiting beliefs are the main cause of most of your suffering and insecurity, and are preventing you from getting the things that you want in life, including healthy, amazing partnership and love. You can have anything you desire, and you would achieve and attract it easily if these hidden things weren't blocking you.

Pandora the love bird

I had a lovebird in college, her name was Pandora. I got her when she was a baby. She was the feistiest bird ever and super smart too. She longed to fly outside. Of course, that was never going to happen for her, but that didn't stop her from trying. She was very good at getting out of her cage. She figured out how to undo the latch so she would get out quite frequently. Once she escaped the confines of her cage, she would fly straight at the big picture window in the living room, hit her little head on the window and become stunned enough to give up. But every time she got out of her cage she would try again. She could see outside to where she wanted to go and just couldn't figure out why she couldn't get there.

Any goal that you have set for yourself but haven't been able to achieve yet is similar to what Pandora experienced. There you see the ideal future with your perfect partner and amazing love, and bam, you fly right into the window. It stops you but you can't see it. That window is just like those invisible beliefs. We can't see them, but they stop us every time from getting what we want.

It will take a little detective work to uncover exactly what these transparent beliefs are that might be running your life. When I work with my clients to figure this out, all I need to do is look at their life experiences as the evidence of their beliefs. Remember from the chart above, we can't experience anything that we don't already believe.

EXERCISE:
What are the patterns?

1. Take a minute or so to float above your life and all of your current or past
    relationships. See if you can notice any patterns. Even if the situations
    were different, are there similar ways that you felt?

    _____

    _____

    _____

    _____

    _____

2. What specifically might you be doing to generate these experiences?

    _____

    _____

    _____

    _____

3. In which ways do these feelings resemble how you felt in your childhood?

    _____

    _____

    _____

    _____

4. Look at these past experiences and start to play detective in your own life.
    Ask yourself this question: "What must I believe about myself in order
    to have these experiences in relationship?" Remember, your beliefs will
    always match your experiences.

    _____

_____

_____

_____

_____

5. If you could let this belief go, what would you have to let go of first?

_____

_____

_____

_____

Where do these beliefs come from?

Long ago and far away, a younger version of you made up a lie about yourself in order to make sense of your world and some things that might have been happening that were painful, scary or dangerous.

Before the age of six, our brains are not capable of making the distinction between what is happening out there and what is happening to you. For example, imagine a little one seeing Mom and Dad fighting. "Uh oh! The two sources of life, the ones I depend on might kill each other! Why is this happening? How can I stop this? And since her little brain can only make it mean something about her, she decides that it is her fault they are fighting. She then swallows a lie about herself: She is not good enough and that is why this whole thing is happening. Now, the good news for her little, scared reptilian brain about swallowing this lie is that if she can just figure out HOW to be good enough then everyone, including herself, will be ok. She now has the illusion that she can control this once uncontrollable situation. TADA! These limiting beliefs we have now saved us back then and that is why they get so stuck!

Be a detective in your own life

At this point, we will be exploring some of our childhood experiences so that we can uncover where some of your core beliefs came from and identify what they are.

As I mentioned before, the only thing we need to do in order to find out what we must believe about ourselves is to look at what we are and what we have been experiencing in our life up to now. To find out where they came from, we need to go back in time.

EXERCISE:
The little girl and her story.

Take a few minutes and complete this writing exercise.

1. What were some of the main emotions I felt consistently as a child?

   _____

   _____

   _____

   _____

   _____

2. How connected did I feel to my mom and what was my experience with her growing up?

   _____

   _____

   _____

   _____

   _____

3. How connected did I feel to my dad and what was my experience with him growing up?

_____

_____

_____

_____

_____

4. What was my parents' relationship like?

_____

_____

_____

_____

_____

5. In response to all of this I felt_____?

_____

_____

_____

_____

_____

6. What might be some of the beliefs that little version of me started to believe about myself, based on what was happening in my childhood?

_____

_____

_____

_____

_____

7. How are these feelings about my childhood affecting me in my relationships and dating experiences?

_____

_____

_____

_____

_____

8. How were my past relationships similar to how I felt as a child? What FEELS the same?

_____

_____

_____

_____

_____

Our brain keeps searching for pain

Not only does the brain love to match patterns and recreate experiences that match our beliefs, but there is a big glitch in the system. There is a part of our brain that feels like it needs to have the pain we survived in the past all the time in order to keep surviving.

For example:
According to the brain, "survival" is equal to what we have lived through already.
It looks something like this:

SURVIVAL   =   WHAT WE HAVE LIVED THROUGH
> Loneliness
> Not feeling loved
> Not feeling important
> Sadness
> Anxiety

So, if survival equals living through all of those negative emotions, the glitch comes in through logical thinking. The brain decides that because it already knows how to survive all of those negative emotions, it must need to keep having those experiences in order to continue to survive.

It would look something like this:

~~SURVIVAL~~   =   WHAT WE LIVED THROUGH
> ~~Loneliness~~
> ~~Not feeling loved~~
> ~~Not feeling important~~
> ~~Sadness~~
> ~~Anxiety~~

Basically, if you stop feeling the negative emotions that you survived as a young one, then your brain fears that it won't survive. It will specifically seek out situations in adulthood that will enable you to continue to experience the pain you felt like when you were a little one. It will do this by picking people or situations to drum up the feelings. Or the brain will utilize its generalization, deletion and distortion techniques so that it can feel the way it needs to in order to survive.

Most of the work I am doing with my clients' neurology is letting the reptilian brain know that happiness is survivable.

....

EXERCISE:
What have you survived?

1. What are some of your survivable emotions? Meaning, what are some of the states you felt as a child?

    _____

    _____

    _____

    _____

    _____

2. Fill in the following chart for yourself. What are some of the main emotions you feel in relationships consistently?

SURVIVAL = WHAT WE HAVE LIVED THROUGH

    _____

    _____

    _____

    _____

    _____

The best thing about uncovering these "survivable" emotions is that now you can see that you—well, your brain at least—is the one picking similar experiences and patterns. This takes you out of the victim role. I remember long ago when I kept running into men who "made" me feel alone all the time. I was sad and angry that *men* were so cold and that for some reason I must not be special enough for them to spend time with me.

However, the realization that my childhood was a long story of a little girl who felt unloved and alone in the world and took me out of the role of being victimized. It gave me the power to begin to heal myself so that I could have different experiences. It was so empowering to finally know that I could change my life, and I didn't have to wait for other people to change. And yes, after focusing on changing some of my past stories and changing my core limiting beliefs about myself, I DID find different kinds of men. And if they were busy, for whatever reason, my brain didn't go to the old default setting of "Oh, that must mean I'm not important." It no longer felt like I was being abandoned.

Your limiting beliefs

We have so many beliefs about love, relationships, men and ourselves. As I mentioned, they are hard to notice sometimes, and the downside is that we often don't realize that we are getting exactly what we believe.

EXERCISE:
Limiting belief fasting

1. Make a list of all the negative beliefs that you have about:
Love

_____

_____

_____

_____

_____

Relationships

_____
_____
_____
_____
_____

Men

_____
_____
_____
_____
_____

Yourself

_____
_____
_____
_____
_____

Loving where you are

We tend to go to war with ourselves when we experience something we don't want. We can make ourselves feel wrong for having the experiences we are having. We can beat ourselves up. We can literally hate our lives when we feel like we are stuck. The common belief around this is, "If I can just hate my experience enough, then I can hate it into changing." This seems logical on some level, however, that kind of problem-solving actually makes things worse. It will make the part of you that is stuck dig its heels in and assert itself even more. Everything that we do or don't do or everything we have or don't have in our lives is that way for a very good reason. The reptilian part of the brain is in charge of keeping us safe and it won't let us have things in our lives that it deems unsafe.

What is your biggest objection to having love?

You can have and be anything that you desire. You can be successful, be confident and have love in your life. If you don't have these things yet, it is because your brain doesn't think it is a good idea to have these things yet. These subconscious objections to what your more logical higher brain wants usually wins out. The reptilian brain's main driver is fear, and the higher prefrontal cortex's driver is love and desire. These two parts of your brain are at war sometimes. Unfortunately, the reptilian part of your brain has seniority. It doesn't care if you are happy; it just wants to make sure you aren't dead. Death always trumps happiness. I mean, who cares if you are happy if you are dead? Sometimes the objections that your brain has to allowing you what you want are very hidden and aren't actually as scary as it thinks. Some people might be afraid that if they let someone in too close, that all of their unlovable parts will be seen and will ultimately be rejected. Maybe if you have love in your life, your deeper fear is that you will have to give something up.

The either/or conflict

My old pattern in relationships was to pick the most unavailable people to get involved with. They were unavailable in many different ways. Some were married or had ex-girlfriends who they weren't over yet. Some were so busy with their jobs or ex-wives and children that I only got the remaining crumbs of their time and attention. Some were players and were good at giving me just enough hope to keep me strung along with the promise of more, but ultimately would never commit. At age thirty-seven I had finally had enough. I was tired of feeling like I wasn't special, not chosen and not a priority.

I had to finally look at what I was doing for these men to show up in my life. It was confusing. I had worked on some of my beliefs already. I didn't feel insecure. I didn't feel like I didn't deserve what I wanted. What was blocking real love from coming into my life was something much, much deeper.

With help, I began to dig down into the deep recesses of my safety patterning to discover a terror of being swallowed up if I was fully in a relationship with somebody. I had grown up with a mentally ill father with undiagnosed borderline personality disorder. The disorder caused him to have dramatic, clingy and intense relationships with the people who were closest to him. He had latched onto me when I was a child, and this pattern continued until I was sixteen years old when I ended my contact with him. He had merged himself with me so tightly that I wasn't allowed to think, feel or do anything that didn't reflect well on him. He needed my attention to feel safe and secure. As a result, what became rooted deep in my brain's safety patterning were my first concepts of love and relationships. Love was suffocating and people use you for their own gain. If you are in a relationship you will lose yourself. The belief that occurred because of this was that I could either have love or I could have myself.

What my brain was brilliantly doing to try and negotiate between the two sides was this: As long as I picked unavailable men I would be able to sort of have a relationship without running the risks of being swallowed up. Simply because they didn't really want to be with me fully, they gave me a lot of space. The problem with this solution is that I was terribly unhappy and unfulfilled in love. It took some time and effort, but easing that pattern in my brain has been the number one challenge that I have had to overcome so far. Fortunately, it was possible to revise with help. These days, I am comfortable letting a relationship in deeply, without the fear of losing all that is me or my own identity. Once that deep fear *and unconscious objection to love shifted, I no longer called unavailable men into my life. I consistently only drew men who wanted to have committed and deep relationships with me. Prior to this shift in myself, when I would occasionally come across an available man who wanted to be with me, I would freak out. I wouldn't let myself love him and would behave in such a way that would eventually get him to walk away from me. I used to say these men were boring, but in fact, they just weren't triggering my survivable emotions of loneliness and not being properly seen.*

EXERCISE:
Giving yourself space and respect

Take a minute to experience what it feels like to not have what you want in a relationship. What is the main emotion that comes up around this? Is it loneliness? Sadness? Anger? Whatever it is, feel it strongly in your body and imagine it growing larger and taking up more space. Can you let it fill your entire body? How about the whole room? How much space does that feeling want to have? Just let it grow as big as it wants and take up as much space as it wants to have. You might notice that when you give it as much space as it desires, it relaxes. You can then thank it for keeping you safe.

Although it feels counterintuitive to fill up your whole space with something that feels so bad, you might have noticed that when you allow that feeling to just be there without resistance, it dissipated. After doing this exercise, some report the feelings disappear altogether or they experience a sensation of becoming allies with them. When we resist how we are feeling, we are disconnected with parts of ourselves. Feeling that our experiences are wrong or trying to stop feeling certain ways will backfire by making the feelings even stronger. Those feelings are there for a reason, and they need to be respected and honored before they can be transformed. When you give your emotions permission to exist, you give yourself permission to also move through them and not get stuck.

Making friends with all of your parts

I am a firm believer that love is just out there. It is like air. We can breathe it in or not. It is a common tendency to blame external circumstances for our inability to create the kind of relationships we want. However, if we do that then we are completely out of control over the situation and nothing will ever change. If we assume there must be a part of you that is not so excited about having a loving relationship, then we can actually work with that.

EXERCISE:
What might you lose when you have love?

Think of the kind of relationship that you want to have. Then ask yourself, "What might I lose that I value when I have this?" The first answer might be "I wouldn't lose anything!" If that is the case for you, then answer this second question.

_____

_____

_____

_____

"What would you have lost as a child if this was different?"

_____

_____

_____

_____

It is important to understand some of the objections that your brain might have about being in a relationship so that we can negotiate a plan that makes all of your parts happy.

You have many parts that make up your whole. As we mentioned earlier, there are parts of us that want one thing and some other parts that seem to intentionally block the things we desire from coming into our lives. There are parts of you in charge of every aspect of your life. We are not always conscious of these parts, but they work with the subconscious to make things happen in your life. Or not. We already know that their main concern is for your safety. These parts were put in charge a long time ago when we were children to keep us safe and happy. They don't tend to update themselves and are most likely operating as if you were still a little one. It is important to make friends with the parts of you that might be objecting to having a healthy, happy relationship. We can imagine that they are there, simply because you don't already have what you want in this area of your life. We can assume these objections are blocking things.

EXERCISE:
Communicating with your parts

This is an NLP exercise that has been around for a very long time that I learned a version of from my trainers at NLP Marin.

1. Take a minute to get comfortable.

2. Close your eyes and imagine an auditorium. Notice that there are plenty of seats and there is also a stage with a podium in front of the room.

3. See yourself as the "senior consciousness," sort of like the boss standing on the stage behind the podium.

4. Imagine that you will be calling a meeting of all of your parts. There are so many parts in charge of all aspects of your life.

5. See them in your mind's eye, filing into the auditorium and sitting down.

6. Once they are all in, give an announcement to all of your parts before you begin the meeting.

7. First, thank them for working so hard to help your life run smoothly. Then let them know that no one is in trouble and no one is getting fired. However, some of them might be up for a promotion if they choose to take it.

8. Now, appeal to the audience, asking the parts that are in charge of blocking you from the relationship that you want to identify themselves.

9. Once they let you know where they are in the crowd, imagine stepping down from the podium and going to join them.

10. Again, thank them for working so hard for you. Make it clear that you know they always have positive intentions for you. Let them know they are not in trouble, nor will they be fired.

11. Ask them if they would be willing to have a quick conversation about their "jobs." See what they say. Most likely they will agree to do so. If, for some reason, they refuse, please just ask them what they need in order to feel safe enough to talk.

12. Ask them if they could take out the original work order from the time when you first put them on the job.

13. Ask them to read the first line of the contract. It will start like this:

"Make sure (Your Name) is _____."
(What is it that they want for you?)

14. Our parts sometimes get stuck in time. Ask them how old that they think you are. If they perceive you as younger then you currently are, let them know how old you really are. This information is sometimes a bit of a shock to them. But the update will be good for them because a lot of the time our parts still think we are young children that need protection.

15. Now ask them, "In your professional opinion, what might have happened to a younger version of me if you had NOT come on the job?"

16. Ask them if they would be willing to do their job of keeping you safe and happy, but if they would be open to trying different ways to protect you— ways that won't keep you from the loving relationship that you want. Ask them to come up with other ways to keep you safe besides their current solution.

17. If they refuse, you can ask them to try it out for two weeks and then you can check back in with them and see how it is going.

18. You might notice that your parts are bored with their jobs and welcome the change.

19. Thank your parts again for being open and willing. You can now come back to the present and open your eyes.

Changing your beliefs will change your experiences

I know that this belief talk might seem gloomy and hopeless. The good news is that beliefs are changeable, even the deep-rooted childhood identity beliefs. NLP work is an excellent modality for getting into the neurology to change these conscious and unconscious patterns and ways that the brain sees ourselves and our reality.

In the meantime, I have an exercise you can do to begin to identify and shift them:

EXERCISE: Live as if....

Once you discover some of the limiting beliefs that you are running in your life, I invite you to play a game of pretending. Pretend as if the opposite were true, and begin to shift your behavior to match up to the opposite belief.

For example, if you have a belief that men are selfish and are dangerous to women, then notice how that might affect the way you walk around in the world. How would you feel around men then? Most likely wary, shy and scared.

What would you do and feel if the opposite were true? Or at least if you shift the belief to be **some** men are scary, but most men are kind and helpful. I bet how you felt and behaved would change.

Another example would be this: let's say you uncovered a deep belief that you felt like you were not good enough. Notice how that belief might affect how you feel and behave. It might cause you to feel insecure, shy or nervous. It might make you feel like you need to prove your worth. It might make you compare yourself to other people. Now, if you pretend that the opposite was true, that you **were** good enough just as you are, I wonder how that would change how you feel? How would it change the way you interact with people? How would it change your confidence level?

Clearing your past

All of your childhood pain, all of your past disappointments in love and all the things that are still affecting you now can seem to be enmeshed with your identity. This means you see yourself based on the things that have happened to you. They begin to feel like they are part of us and not separate from who we really are. We can over-identify with trauma and negative experiences and let them shape how we see ourselves and how we behave. The sad part of that is these past traumas become our prisons as we keep re-living them over and over. When we are still carrying them with us they can become a false identity. Your brain will often grab onto negative past experiences and create a matrix and filter through how you see yourself, love and possibilities based on the past. The past is already done, but as you see the world and love based on that filter, you will only be able to create and keep having those same experiences. You will need to release all the negative things that you are basing your present and future on so that you can have a clean slate.

The good news is that the future is just the past moving through you now. Think of your desire for love as something that has already manifested and imagine that the future is just sending you glimpses of what has already happened so you can be excited about it now.

....

Meditation:
Releasing what no longer serves you

Get comfortable. Close your eyes. Begin by feeling your breath coming in and out. Breathe in and breathe out. Gently. Effortlessly. Allow your heart to open and unlock. Feel your hips unwinding. Relax your body and letting life flow through you, allowing you to move forward. Giving gratitude for your body and all it does to support you each and every day. Now that you are relaxed, imagine that you are standing next to the sea. You see that the water is calm and pristine. You begin to step into the water and notice that the water isn't too cold or too warm. It is just perfect. As you continue wading in the water, walking down the empty beach, you come across a dock, and the end of this dock you see a boat tied to it. You step up on the dock. You begin to walk toward the boat. As you get closer to it, you notice that this boat has your name on it. You become aware that this boat is here just for you. You hear a voice say, "Unload everything that is no longer serving you."

You unlock your heart and search it for any and all people, situations or incidences that have been weighing you down and dampening your soul. Take these thoughts, people, experiences and put all of them into the boat. Begin to fill the boat with everything that's been holding you back as well as any toxic experiences that keep you from moving forward, childhood memories and anything else you have been holding onto. Load up all painful moments and all the people that have hurt you in any way. As you keep filling the boat, you notice there is plenty of room for it all. Take your time and make sure you get all of them out of your heart and into the boat.

As you continue to place them in the boat, thank each experience. Those challenges have allowed you to grow. They are beautiful in their own right, because without them you wouldn't have had a chance to grow.

When you are finished placing all of them in the boat, slowly untie the rope that has been holding the boat in place and anchored to the dock. Watch as the boat drifts slowly from the dock into the sea. As it gets farther and farther away, wave to it with gratitude. Say, "Thank you for being a guide for me. Thank you for my growth," knowing this will be the last time that these things will be shrouding your true spirit. Watch the boat get farther and farther away until it finally disappears out of sight. You may feel grief as you let some of these things and people go, but the grief is appropriate. They are done. They have passed on. *The future is just the past moving through you now.* Your grief will transform *now* into a sense of freedom and release. You will *now* feel a sense of lightness. Take a moment to feel the new space that is in you, now that these things have left you. There is room for new, amazing things to come in. Now say to yourself silently, "I am open to receive, I am free. I am light. I am love...... I AM love." Remember who you are now that all of these past experiences and people are no longer shrouding you.

Remember who you are.

Your life has given you only as much as you can handle. At times, it may seem like too much, and you may have doubt about your abilities to deal with certain things, and yet you have done it. Your soul has set sail into your life to learn. But don't forget home.

Now gently bring yourself back into your body and into the room. Feel free to take some time to write down anything that may have come up for you during the meditation.

_____

_____

_____

_____

_____

_____

_____

_____

_____

_____

4

Letting Go of the Family Pain

You have already seen how your own experiences in life and childhood can affect your belief system and the safety patterning in the brain that can keep you stuck.

There is another not so fun and interesting way that our brain can block us from having the love that we want in our lives. It is rooted in the concept of the "family soul" or "generational pain." Bert Hellinger, a German psychotherapist, is famous for revolutionizing family therapy by illuminating the unconscious loyalties within families through his method known as Family Constellations. Hellinger has observed that traumatic events, such as the premature death of a parent, sibling or child, an abandonment, crime, suicide, abuse, money issues, loss of fortune, and being exiled from your country all can exert a powerful force, affecting later generations. Entangled with unhappiness from the past, family members often continue patterns of anxiety, depression, anger, guilt, fear, chronic illness and unfulfilled relationships.

Quite often we find ourselves in a pattern of loyalty with our families, and this can even go back generations. These patterns can show up as a direct replica of their past situation or as a metaphorical repeat. This is happening way back in our subconscious minds and is done out of love for them and out of the safety of belonging in the "pack," so to speak.

We still have wiring in our brains that is busy searching to replicate what the pack does in order to survive. For instance, if a bunny didn't learn to run away from foxes, then its survival would be at stake. Not only does a bunny observe the other bunnies running from predators, but that instinct is also hardwired in their neurology and passed down to offspring as a way to preserve the species. We share similar wiring even though we have high-functioning, rational brains that can say, "Of course I can have it better than my parents." Quite often, I will see people subconsciously holding themselves back in areas that were tough or didn't work out for their parents, grandparents or older siblings.

Often, when people can't seem to find love or when they keep finding themselves in painful relationships, we can look to the generations before and see similar pain.

We can latch on to their pain in the hopes of making them better or as a way to belong with them. These unconscious contracts can wreak havoc in our lives today and keep us blocked, lonely, unhappy and miserable.

I won't have love because you didn't

Kim was a stunning, charming woman in her mid-forties. She dated off and on but could never find a man who she wanted to get serious with. Plenty of men wanted her, but she would always find something wrong with them and end the brief dating periods. When I was working with her, we uncovered that at a certain point in the dating process, every time she felt like she was going to give in and fall for someone, it felt as if a strong force would pull her back. She would wake up the next day feeling disenchanted with the man and end up breaking it off. Doing Family Constellation work with her, I discovered that her older brother died in a car accident on the way to his wedding. Kim, being fifteen at the time, was devastated by the loss of her big brother. Her subconscious mind had aligned herself with his loss and somehow she vowed to never have love in her life either. So, every time she got close, she would pull back and end it, just as her brother was pulled into death and didn't get to fulfill his love desire either.

I will have your pain:

Helen was recovering from an abusive marriage. When she sat down in my office she was beside herself with wonder at how she had gotten herself into this situation. "I came from a good home. Both of my parents were loving, and I never even got spanked as a child. How did I end up here?" she cried. Doing some family background exploration, I uncovered that her mother was abused as a child by her own father. She was beaten daily and had vowed that when she had children she was going to raise them with kindness. Not only that, she was going to pick a gentle man to be the father of her children. She did just that. She was so acutely aware of her parenting, ensuring that she did a better job than her own parents, but it didn't work. What Helen's system had done was to align herself with her mom's abuse and she subconsciously picked a man who was abusive so that she could repeat her mother's trauma. Not only that but if she picked an abusive man then in a weird way, it made her grandfather innocent.

We are connected in our pain:

Before I transformed my own love patterns, I had the distinct experience of never trusting men to stick around, even though I had never been abandoned or broken up with by anyone. In fact, I was usually the one to leave my relationships. I also had a pervasive sense of feeling alone. I felt alone in life no matter who I was with, no matter how many friends I had or whether I was married or single. I was just alone.

My nana on my father's side grew up in the Netherlands. When she was eight years old, her father's greenhouse business went bankrupt. This was back in the year 1911 and bankruptcy in those days meant you lost everything! They lost the house, and the five children were sent away all over the country to be cared for by relatives. My eight-year-old nana was sent far away to live with distant cousins whom she had never met before. Meanwhile, her father decided to set sail for the new world, to the United States, promising to find a job, make money and send for his family once he got settled. Long story short, a year went by and her father was enjoying sight-seeing in the new country and was not that eager to make money. My great-grandmother finally borrowed money from her family to get the children and herself to the U.S. to be reunited with her husband.

As you can see, my experience was very similar to my nana's experience. I felt like I was going to be left and abandoned and so I never trusted men. In the deepest part of me, my sense of being alone was rooted my nana's own abandonment issues from the time she was all alone, away from her family, not knowing if they were ever going to come and get her.

Now that you might be getting an idea of how this can play out, the other question is HOW to make it stop. The first thing is to uncover what might be playing out as you did in the above exercises. The next thing is to acknowledge that you belong to a group or family simply because of your DNA. You don't have to belong by repeating their pain or being like them. Your belonging is already a given, so you don't have to keep proving it. The next thing is to understand is that no matter how much you try to deprive yourself of love or things that you really want in your life, you will NEVER be able to fix it for your family, your parents or your ancestors. No amount of suffering now will make it better for them back then.

EXERCISE:
Releasing the family pain

1. When you think of your love life and the patterns in it, who (either living or dead) comes to mind who didn't get love/family or relationship that he or she must have wanted?

_____

_____

_____

_____

_____

2. Get a sense of whoever pops up first even if you don't know for sure. You will have an impression of it. A name, impression or image will pop up.

_____

_____

_____

_____

_____

3. What did that person want that he or she didn't get?

_____

_____

_____

_____

_____

4. In what ways is your life similar?

_____

_____

_____

_____

_____

5. How much longer will you throw yourself under the bus to help this person? Will it really help?

_____

_____

_____

_____

_____

Visualization:

Step into a version of yourself standing in front of the family member who popped up. In your mind say to this person, "I love you so much. I wanted to fix your life and your pain for you, but I didn't know how. I decided to have all of your pain with you so I could absorb it from you, and if that didn't work, at least we would be bonded together through our pain."

Now imagine yourself stepping into the person in front of you and notice his or her reaction to what you just said. What does he or she want most for you? Hear them say, "You may not have my pain and you do me no honor in trying to take it from me. It does my heart good to see you doing well and having love in your life, even if I could not."

Please take a minute to write down any of your thoughts and ideas that have come up around this.

_____

_____

_____

_____

_____

Hall of women ancestors

Ellen had come to me after she had found out her husband of twenty years was having an affair. She admitted that this wasn't the first time and that over the course of their marriage, he had often "fallen in love" with other women. He was an artist, he would explain to her, and he couldn't help that he loved beautiful women. He would always beg her forgiveness and profess his undying love for her so she always stayed.

This time, however, she had already been doing NLP belief change work with me and her self-esteem had gotten stronger. She was feeling powerful and knew deep down in her soul that she was worth being treated with respect. So this time she was going to walk away for good. I saw the pain in her eyes as she told me this. She truly did love her husband, but she also loved herself now, and she was no longer going to abuse herself by staying with him through this chronic disregard and disrespect.

As she was going through her process, she had a dream about all the women, generations back, on her mother's side who had also had cheating, disrespectful men in their lives. Every single one of them stayed and put up with the bad behavior from their husbands. The fact that Ellen was leaving her marriage sent her system into a panic at first. She was sort of a pioneer. Subconsciously, she felt a loyalty to the pain of the woman she had come from, and in a way, it felt like a betrayal to be the one to finally get away, to claim a better life and declare that she deserved better. We did some work around this and she realized that all of the women generations back who were abused by the men in their lives would actually be ecstatic that she was going to have it better. They were cheering her on. She left her husband and created a brand new powerful bright life for herself. She met another man a year later who treated her like a queen. She would have never let such a man into her life if she hadn't let go of the subconscious loyalty to the family pain.

5

The You in the We

One of the most common complaints I hear from the women I work with is that they feel like they "lose themselves" in a relationship. What does this mean? It means that they stop doing things that make them happy and they focus all of their energy on their man or the relationship. Or they stop speaking up for themselves. They might just agree with their partner on everything or they might stop asking for things that they want for fear of rocking the boat or being rejected in some way.

In the F.L.I.R.T. Course, we spend a lot of time discussing how "radiance" is a huge factor in attraction. This is true not only in finding a relationship but in keeping it alive and having your man be consistently attracted to you. Radiance in a woman happens when she is filled up. It happens when she is living her life in joy. It happens when she no longer needs a man to complete her life and she is walking around in love with herself and her life. At this point, men often say they become mesmerized with a woman and she is compelling to be around. She draws them in like a magnet and has an inner glow or vibrancy that we call *radiance*. It is one of the main feminine qualities that makes a woman very attractive.

Some women possess this magnetizing radiance before they meet their partners, but once they become attached they slowly give up their passions and the other things that keep them fully embracing life. Not only does this result in their men losing some interest in them, but because these women are often acquiescing to their partners' needs and not standing up for their own, the men might even start to take them for granted. Often women will start to give up their passions and interests and begin to follow their partners' interests. It is fine to be exposed to new things and activities but not to replace your own with them. Many women report eventually becoming resentful of their partners as if they somehow took away the lives they had loved, even though the women themselves were the ones giving these things away. It is true that some sacrifices must be made in relationships, but the things that truly make you happy are not the ones to sacrifice.

Some women have a secret agenda when searching for a relationship. They are looking for a relationship so they can be happy. The big problem is if there is an empty space in your life that you are hoping someone else will fill for you, then you are going out in the world with a sense of not being whole and you will most likely attract a partner who is not whole either. You might not have the clarity to really see if someone is a good fit because you are feeling like you "need" someone. At that point, almost anyone will do and this is a recipe for disaster.

Men have a strong desire to make the women they are with happy. When the woman a man is with is happy, he deems himself successful and accomplished. When he meets a woman who is already happy, he is naturally more attracted to her because his job will be easier and he has more of an opportunity to be successful at this. Besides this, it is always more pleasurable to be around positive, happy people than the opposite. If he meets someone who can't make herself happy, he registers that this will be a hard job, and not only that but he might even fail. Failing at making the woman he is with happy will make him feel less attracted and not as excited to be with her.

We will talk more about men and their view of relationships later, but this is a good thing to remember: Men want to win. The way they win in love is if their partners are happy. If they are winning, they will want to continue. If they can't win, they will eventually give up and leave.

Men also have a deep-seated need for freedom and an aversion to being bogged down. We will also talk more about this later, but when a woman *needs* a man to make her happy, what happens for him deep in his subconscious is that he will be afraid of losing a lot of his own freedoms because she needs him too much. To sum it all up: a woman who is full and happy is confident and attractive. A woman who is lacking and looking for love to fill her up is a liability.

The most powerful place that a woman can occupy in her life is to be fully in love with her life and full of joy, even if she hasn't found her partner yet. Before I met my current partner, I came to a point in my life where I felt complete and happy even though I was single. It took a lot of attention and energy to finally create a life that I felt joyful and content in. I recall saying to a girlfriend of mine, "My life is so awesome right now that whoever I meet better make my life better or at least not kill my joy." From that place, because things were already good, I was very choosy about what or who I was going to let into my life. This was because I didn't *need* a partner. I *wanted* one.

EXERCISE:
Losing yourself

1. What does it feel like when you lose yourself in a relationship?

_____

_____

_____

_____

_____

2. What are some of the things you have given up or stopped doing when you've been in a relationship?

_____

_____

_____

_____

_____

3. What were the bigger consequences of this?

_____

_____

_____

_____

EXERCISE:
What do you love

1. Make a list of all the things that give you joy and pleasure. Make the list juicy and exciting.

_____

_____

_____

_____

2. After you make the list of things that give you joy, make a note of the last time that you did that particular thing.

_____

_____

_____

_____

....

EXERCISE:
30 Days of self-love challenge

Take your list and arrange the activities into 3 categories.

Category 1- Things that can be done in 5 minutes

Category 2-Things that can be done in 30 minutes

Category 3-Things that can be done in an hour or longer

For the next thirty days, make a commitment to yourself to do at least one thing on your list EVERY DAY. It takes only twenty-eight days to create a habit. Making a commitment to take care of yourself and your need for pleasure will also begin to put pressure on some of those limiting beliefs that we have previously worked on. If you have limiting beliefs it is usually hard to commit to doing good things for yourself. By making this commitment and doing the things that give you pleasure, you are going against what the belief would have you do; therefore, it puts pressure on the belief simply by behaving differently.

When you are filling up your life with pleasure, it will begin to feel fuller. You will start feeling happier, and not only will you be able to pick a better partner for yourself, but your happiness will radiate and you will become more attractive. People want to be around people who are living life to the fullest; they want to be a part of that. When your life feels full, you will radiate to the men who you meet, "I have an amazing life. Care to join me?"

Think about the last time you saw a stranger who looked happy. How did you feel around this person? Now, think about the last time you saw a stranger who looked like he or she was not happy or maybe had a look on his or her face that screamed, "Leave me alone."

Humans are more attuned to the moods of other people than we realize, and we react to each other based on this subtle energy. If you are walking around with resting "grumpy" face, most likely no one will want to approach you. Believe it or not, men are afraid of rejection, especially when it comes to approaching women. They need to feel that the risk of being turned away is minimal. When they see a woman who looks happy, the chances of rejection seem to go down. Happy women are more likely to be approached and asked out.

The best way to look happy is to actually **BE** happy! Make cultivating your own pleasure and joy your number one priority and things will begin to change dramatically for you in all areas of your life, not just in relationships.

Foul weather friend

We have all experienced the girlfriend who disappears once she starts dating someone. The once a week get-together turns into once a month or once every other month. You used to talk every week and now you barely hear from her, and when you do it is because you reached out. When she was single and lonely you were her priority, and now you have been tossed aside. Not only is it annoying and hurtful, but also not a good thing for her budding relationship. It is normal to want to spend more and more time with a love interest in the beginning, but forgetting to give energy to the rest of your life and other relationships is a no-no.

Your friends are a part of your life that should still get equal attention even when you have a new love interest. If you have close friends, then you will always feel supported and you won't need to get everything from your partner which, by the way, is impossible. Your friends will always be there for you. Your relationships might come and go, but a good friendship can last forever. Resist the urge to put those friends on the back burner when you are falling in love, and you will remain whole.

Do you love and give too much?

There are plenty of ways in which women tend to throw the balance off in giving and taking by giving too much in a relationship. Sometimes "giving" looks like you are being kind and loving. But often the motivation comes from being scared and insecure, driven by the fear that if you aren't giving or valuable to your partner, that he won't love you or he will leave. This is going back to those limiting beliefs that we spoke of earlier. There is frequently a hope that your partner will love you more if you are "doing" things for him. Sometimes giving too much is sneaky and hard to see. It could look something like being preoccupied with your man's issues or dramas. Or it could be making sure you are taking care of your partner all the time and being eager to help him. Maybe you are the one to always call or plan the dates. Being the only one buying gifts or tokens of love or being the only one initiating quality time also falls into the category of giving too much.

Some of the women who share with me the extreme efforts they put into their relationships feel tired and drained. They also never really know if their guys are into them because they are doing all the emotional work in the relationship, not allowing their partners to make any effort or be able to offer any tokens of love. They are scared to stop "doing" because they are afraid the men won't pick up the slack. They are usually not sure of their own value if they aren't giving. The problem with this kind of unbalanced giving is that it causes an unhealthy dynamic in the relationship. Humans have an inner sense of reciprocity. When someone gives, we have a natural urge to give back. In a relationship where someone is always giving, it is difficult for the other person to catch up to balance the score. When this happens, the receiver begins to feel a sense of guilt. He (or she) might not be aware of it at first, but eventually, he might become resentful of the giving or he might not want to be in the relationship anymore because it is causing him to feel bad.

As I mentioned before, people are pretty aware of the subtleties of intention. When we are giving to people out of a sense of fear or lack of self-worth or because we want something back, that intention is felt by the other person and it doesn't feel good. It leaves the receiver feeling obligated and not appreciative.

Giving and receiving

My friend once told me that for the first year she was with her boyfriend, she would get upset and uncomfortable when he would open the door for her.

Marissa was not an old-school feminist, so I asked her why this made her uncomfortable. She told me that when people did nice things for her she always felt guilty, especially if it seemed like they went out of their way for her.

Marissa, on the other hand, went out of her way for a lot of people. She is kind and caring, but her inability to receive was messing up the balance in her relationships.

When the balance between giving and receiving is in perfect flow in a relationship, you can't tell who is giving and who is receiving. There is a balance. When both people are giving and receiving equally, it becomes a beautiful dance.

Women in general, tend to give more than they are comfortable receiving, thus throwing off the healthy equilibrium in relationships. As a result, they are left feeling depleted and eventually resentful. Believe it or not, this makes the other person feel guilty. There is a natural law of reciprocity with human beings. When someone gives, we tend to want to give back to even the score. That is why the way the Easter Seals' method is an excellent way to raise money. They send you preprinted address labels for free, saying, "It is our gift to you." Then they state, "If you would like to make a donation here is where you send it."

Now, you have three options. 1) You can use the labels without donating and then feel a little guilty every time you use one because you didn't give anything back. 2) You can send in a donation to relieve your guilt. 3) You can just throw them away because, "Hey! I didn't ask for these, how dare you make me feel guilty?"

If you tend to give more than you let yourself receive in a relationship, then most likely you are making the other person feel guilty because he can never even the score. Those guilty feelings will be associated with being around you. And eventually, it won't feel very good to be around you anymore.

A man who has a healthy relationship with his masculine energy wants to give and provide. When he feels needed and appreciated, he will most likely feel great being around you. If you can't receive, then he can't get what he needs to stay attracted to you, which is being of service.

Here are some ways that women give too much in relationships:

You buy your man presents more often than he buys you presents.
You plan most dates.
You do most of the calling and keeping up contact.
You worry and are preoccupied with his life and little problems he might be having.
You try to solve these problems for him.
You refuse to let him pay for things.
You refuse his help.

Susanne was preoccupied with her boyfriend's job search. Joe was unemployed and had been looking for a job off and on for a few months. Susanne spent every bit of her extra time when she wasn't at her own demanding job searching for jobs for Joe. She helped him write his resume and began sending them into companies without his knowledge. When she came to see me, Joe was threatening to break up with her. She couldn't understand why he wanted to leave after all she had done for him.

Joe was overwhelmed with Susanne's "help," and he felt unable to help her back. Not only that but it felt to him like she didn't trust him to handle his own affairs.

When working with her, we uncovered that this excessive helping tended to be a pattern in her relationships. "I just get overinvolved with their lives," she said.

When I asked her what positive result she was hoping to gain by being so help-ful, she paused for a moment to consider the question. "Well, honestly," she said, with downturned eyes, "I feel that if I am helpful, then they will come to rely on me and then they won't leave me."

That revelation was the beginning of Susanne's healing journey toward healthy, interdependent love, as well as a first step in unwinding the deeper belief that she was only lovable if she were valuable to someone.

Some other reasons why women tend to give too much:

They feel that it is the only way to get people to like them.

They are natural caregivers.

They don't trust their partners to get things done, so they do it themselves.

They have low self-esteem and negative beliefs about themselves, and they feel it is the only way to be valuable.

EXERCISE:
What are you giving too much of?

1. Make a list of some of the things that you might be taking on that aren't your responsibility in your current or past relationships.

    _____

    _____

    _____

    _____

    _____

2. List some of the things that you do most of in your past relationships without your partner returning the energy back.

_____

_____

_____

_____

_____

These are the things that are most likely unbalanced in your relationships.

EXERCISE:
What are you getting by giving too much?

1. Write about the positive things that come as a result of over-giving or being too involved with your partners' problems. What are you trying to gain by being so helpful or by giving all that you do?

_____

_____

_____

_____

_____

What might happen if you stop?

_____

_____

_____

_____

_____

6

Understanding Your Man
"Learning Man Speak"

Getting the MAN-U-AL

Most of the women I know find men confusing at some point. It seems like a cosmic joke that we are to mate with them when they seem like complete alien creatures sometimes. One of the reasons for this disconnect is that our female brains function differently than theirs. This difference in processing can cause a major conflict between the sexes, especially when it comes to love relationships.

Because of these differences, it is important to learn what I call "Man Speak." If you learn the language of men and learn how they see love and life, you will gain a much better understanding, which will bring more harmony to your relationships. Please know that I am not an advocate of contorting yourself so that you can be what men want. There are relationship coaches and dating programs out there that try to sell that kind of bull pucky such as, "How to Get Him to Commit," or "10 Things You are Doing Wrong That Drive Men Away," etc. The theory that tells a woman she needs to be something else to make a man want her, or that she needs to understand him so that she can manipulate him into commitment, is damaging to the already abused feminine spirit. I will never tell you to be something you are not. I will never tell you to change or be better. Besides, why the heck would you want to be with a man who you had to coerce into committing to you? All these courses and coaches only perpetuate the feelings that women already have about not being good enough and needing to be someone else in order to get love. I say, "Forget that!" You are already fine just as you are. You don't need to change a thing nor do you need to cater to men as if they are stupid or have fragile, delicate egos that you can damage. Let's just forget all that nonsense.

However, I do think it is important to understand men, their filters and how they think and feel about relationships because it is going to help you get more of what YOU want in love. Think about it as if you were going to a foreign country. It is often useful to learn a few key phrases of the native language or to learn something about the culture to make your experience easier. Grab your passport and get ready for a journey. Welcome to the mysterious land, uncharted by most women: Man Land.

EXERCISE:
What is a man?

You might have never pondered this question before. However, it is useful to look at what some of your attitudes and perceptions of men are. Take a minute or so and write down what comes to mind.

_____

_____

_____

_____

_____

EXERCISE:
What are the differences between men and women?

1. Take some time to write your thoughts here: Are all men the same? If not, what are some of the similarities that you see?

_____

_____

_____

_____

_____

2. Are all women the same? If not, what are some of the similarities that you
    see?

_____

_____

_____

_____

Of course, men and women are individuals, but as a group, I do believe
that women have certain needs and that men as a whole have a lot in common
with each other as well, especially when it comes to how they think, act, feel
and what they need to feel appreciated. Everything I will write here is based
on years of research and direct observation of the men I have worked with and
have been in relationships with. I have taken into account views from experts
in attraction, psychology, evolution, biology and more.

It will be valuable for you to understand the common differences between
the sexes.

The male brain versus the female brain

The masculine brain is physically different from the female brain in many
ways that explain why both men and women have been frustrated with each
other and feel lost when it comes to understanding one another. It is common

that we relate and respond to others as if they were like us. Meaning this: when someone does something you would never do or doesn't do something that you would naturally do or pay attention to, it can be baffling. It is common to judge others' behavior based on what you would do or not do. And when it comes to men versus women there are just some things that will be more challenging for each side, both mentally and emotionally.

The corpus callosum

This is the bridge of nerve tissue that connects the right and left sides of the brain. If you look at images of a male brain versus a female brain, you will see that there are more nerves that connect the two hemispheres in a female brain. It is also thought that females have language functioning on both sides of the brain whereas a male only has language functioning on one side. So, in simple terms, females can use both hemispheres at once when speaking. They can feel, identify and talk about how they are feeling all at the same time. The male brain cannot.

This explains why, when you are having a serious discussion with your guy and you ask him how he feels about something, he says, "I don't know." It is because he really doesn't know. It's not that he is emotionally stunted. He isn't being elusive or difficult: he just needs to take a minute or a day so that he can manually go over to his emotional part and figure out what he is feeling and then he can come back a report to you what he found.

So often fights and misunderstandings have occurred simply because a woman feels like her guy is just being insensitive or doesn't really care. He does. He just can't talk about it and feel it at the same time.

Think back to some of your past or present-day experiences. Now that you know more about how the male brain works, how will that change the way you see things or how you deal with them?

Multi-Tasking versus Single-Minded Focus

The female brain is wired to be an excellent multi-tasker. It is more relationally focused. It can see all the parts of a whole and how they relate to the other parts. This is why women often seem to be better at planning than men.

The male brain is designed to be hyper-focused on one task at a time until completion. The beauty of this is that it is hard to distract the male brain from its task until it is completed, whereas the female brain can get distracted easily. It is like working on your computer. The female brain will have all windows open at once and flip from one to another. The male brain, on the other hand, is like having one window open at a time, doing what you need to do in that window and then closing it before you open the next one. A slew of arguments and frustrations can arise just because of the multi-window versus the single window mindset in men and women. Here are some examples of how this can go frustratingly wrong: You sent a text to your boyfriend over two hours ago and he isn't getting back to you. What do you usually make this mean?

We as women can text someone, check our email, talk to our girlfriends and eat our lunch all at the same time. Remember the relational quality of the female brain can hold everything at once. When you text your partner, he might be intensely focusing on something. He has forgotten about you for the time being, and he most likely won't respond until he is finished with his task. Be patient and don't make it mean that he is ignoring you or cheating on you or whatever other bad thing you make it mean.

What happens when a man is focusing on something and someone tries to get his attention or interrupts? Men have described that it feels like someone sticking out their foot and tripping them when they are running a race. It is that jarring and unpleasant.

Having a female relational brain also means that we might prioritize relationships more than our male counterparts. The relational brain is in tune with other people's needs and emotions and is better at recognizing our own and others' emotions. Because we are so good at it, we can get a little miffed at our male partners who seem like they don't track our needs very well. They might not be in touch with how we are feeling all of the time. They require us to tell them how we are feeling, unlike our girlfriends who seem to naturally perceive how we feel and what we need. Because relationships are more of a focus for the female brain, when things aren't going well in that area of their life or there is a conflict, it will seem to be the only thing that matters. If your relationship isn't right, your life doesn't feel right.

For our singly focused male friends, thinking and analyzing are their brains' strong suits. Systematizing and figuring out HOW things work are the goals. The purpose of this problem solving is to understand and predict the system for success, AKA survival. Emotions don't really play that big of a part here. That isn't to say that your guy is void of emotions, but it just isn't his main channel of information processing. I am not saying that your man doesn't care about your relationship; it just isn't his *main* priority. For him, usually his main priorities are success, purpose, and direction. When things are not going well for him in these areas, his life feels out of balance. When things are not going well in his love relationship, it is just a problem to analyze and fix. Men see everything in the world as a problem to solve. Remember, they look at things through the filter of, "Am I winning or am I losing?" We will talk more about this in later chapters. Are you beginning to see why these two very different ways of seeing the world and relationships can become a comedy of errors between the sexes at some point?

Before you take offense at any of this, please know that the human body and brain are designed for survival. The male brain's single-minded focus and the fact that it's a bit cut off from emotion is an excellent survival skill when hunting and or fighting in battle. If you are out for days hunting not only for your survival but for your tribe's survival, being able to stay focused will be an excellent skill to have in order for you to be successful. If you are in combat, having empathy or being in touch with your own emotions would make it difficult to do what you have to do to survive.

The female relational brain, on the other hand, is wired for survival through multi-tasking and tuning into the needs of her young. Historically speaking, survival was also based on being in tune with the rest of the females in the tribe. They relied on each other as the men were often gone or at risk of dying while hunting or in battle. If you have to watch the children, watch out for lions and make food for your tribe, being able to multi-task and keep track of all of it at once would be the best survival skill you could have. Being able to anticipate the needs of your young would also help you be more successful in taking care of them efficiently. As you begin to see the evolutionary reasons why men and women are different, we can begin to work with and understand each other's strengths and differences.

The problem comes when women want men to be more like women and men want women to be more like men. A woman may complain that her man isn't emotional enough or present enough. She becomes frustrated when he won't share his emotions with her. A man may complain that his woman is too emotional. He feels like she wants to process things too much and he wishes she could just enjoy the moment without having to know exactly how he is feeling all the time. Where can we find balance within these differences? Is there a way to draw your man out into deeper intimacy without pushing him so much? Is there a way for men to learn how to go deeper naturally? Is there a way for women to be content with NOT processing sometimes and just trusting that everything is okay?

We won't fundamentally be able to change these things. That said, everything and everyone is on a spectrum. There are some men who are more comfortable with their emotions, and the same goes for women who aren't always as comfortable. It is best to find what works for you, learn to appreciate the differences and not take them personally.

EXERCISE:
What do you admire?

What is something you can admire about the male brain?

_____

_____

_____

_____

_____

What is something you cherish about your female brain?

_____

_____

_____

_____

_____

Masculine pretense

All little boys think about and look forward to growing up to be men. There are a set of attitudes they feel they need to have and certain ways they want to be seen in the world in order to be viewed as a real man. It is important for them that they are seen as strong, independent, free and in control.

It might appear that nothing can hurt a man emotionally and that people can't move him deeply either, although this is just a PRETENSE. Beneath these false perceptions, men are afraid of being alone and are in need of intimacy and love just as much as we are. Love is difficult for them because they feel like they need to keep up these pretenses. They need to be strong, not emotional. They can't be needy or seen as weak. They can't let people in as easily.

There are also some basic needs that all men have in relationships that are different than your needs. His openness to commit to you and be with you is based on how you deal with these four basic needs. If you trigger fear in one of these areas, or if you support him in these areas, he will either have a positive or negative gut reaction to you and act accordingly. His readiness to commit to you reflects on how you, as a woman, handle these needs.

1. The need to be special

You might not realize this, but men are often judged by their status in the world, not just by women they date but by everyone. They are their job, they are their income and they are their accomplishments. It is a rare thing for them to be really seen up close and personal as an individual. When I say that a man wants to feel special, I mean that in a very particular way. We all want to feel special, but men often don't have the same opportunities in the world as we do to do so.

If you appreciate him in a personal way, you will have already piqued his interest. Men often complain to me that their first dates feel like interviews for either sugar daddy or sperm donor. They feel like they are being vetted for a future role and not being seen as a unique person. This mimics their experience with the rest of the world.

If you see him as a unique individual and try to get to know him personally, then you are already ahead of the game. By really seeing him as a unique individual and encouraging him to share his true self, you will be creating a bond and rapport that he doesn't get to experience with many people.

If you become the woman who not only lets a man be himself but also wants to know what matters to him, you will become very special to him, freeing him from the personal imprisonment of not revealing himself.

When getting to know a man on a first date, at all costs, avoid those examining interview questions:

What do you do for a living?

Where do you live?

Do you want children?

And so forth.

These are innocent enough questions but 1) they don't promote connection and 2) they can feel like probing questions designed to gauge his status in the world. These make men feel like they are being quizzed and judged as to whether or not they are husband/boyfriend material. With this line of questioning, they will not feel special at all. By asking a man more connecting questions, you are letting him know that you want to see him as he truly is, not how he looks on paper, and that will make you special to him. In addition, this is an amazing way to build a connection with anyone, not just a man. Ask questions that are designed to encourage him to reveal himself in a safe and fun way. For example, it's not a great idea to ask, "So you're a lawyer, huh?" (This sounds like you are fishing for how much money he makes.) Instead, you can ask what inspired him to become a lawyer or what is the most rewarding thing about his job. You will learn so much more about the man in front of you with these kinds of connecting questions.

If you notice something that he is good at or you admire in him, let him know that you notice. He will begin to feel really seen by you for his uniqueness and not just because he is filling a role of "man" in your life. When he starts to trust that you won't take his freedom away or be critical of him, he will reveal more about himself as the relationship goes on.

2. The need for freedom

It is not unusual for a man to have an irrational fear that his freedom is always at stake. He has spent his whole life as a little boy, waiting to be a grown man who is in control of his own decisions, his own time, his own money and the free will to be able to do what he wants. He tends to be very nervous about being tied down and having his freedom and autonomy taken away. Because of this, it is important for him to understand that being with you does not mean emasculation or imprisonment. He will be watchful about how much of his life he will need to give up and what he won't be able to do if he is with you. Will he still be able to go out with the guys? Will he still be able to have his man cave? Will he be bossed around or will he still be able to have a say in his life and your relationship?

Quite often the fear is rational and based on reality. The old ball and chain joke isn't really a joke. Unfortunately, it comes from a history of women coming into men's lives and trying to change them. Women often feel like they need to refine men, monitor them and make them different and more palatable for partnership.

If your man senses that you are needy or insecure, this will also set off the "no freedom" alarm bells. Let me put it this way: a man wants to be useful, but if he is being clung to as a woman's only source of happiness and she doesn't have her own life, he will begin to feel too responsible for her happiness. This translates as a loss of freedom. When you have your own life, friends, hobbies and things that make you happy outside of your relationship, not only are you a more well-rounded person for yourself, you will be a much better partner and won't trigger the loss of freedom in your man.

Jealousy will also trigger the "loss of freedom button" in men. If you are jealous of his friends, other women or things he does without you, you are putting limits on him. Now, seriously, if you have an agreement that you are monogamous, you need to trust that he will honor that agreement. If you don't trust him, is this because of *your* insecurities? Or is he giving you a reason not to trust him? If he is not trustworthy then you really need to go back to your compass list and ask yourself why you would want to be with a man you don't trust.

3. The need for loyalty

This might seem like a strange concept. Of course, if you are in a relationship you will be loyal, right? I am not talking about flirting or sleeping with other men. There is a certain kind of loyalty that your man is looking for. To boil it down, he needs to feel like he is a hero. Remember, he wants to be seen in the eyes of the world as a strong, in-control man. He wants to be seen by others in a good light.

I will give you two examples of how this can go very wrong in relationship.

Mary was at a dinner party with her husband Fredrick. During dinner, the subject of work and almost getting fired was brought up by one of the guests. Mary chimed in, playfully chiding her husband as she told everyone how he almost got fired from his job recently because of the dumb mistake he made on a project. Mary's tone was light and playful but the look on Fredrick's face was horrified. She had brought to the public's attention something private and embarrassing and she wasn't backing him up.

Please be mindful of protecting his public image. Don't share personal information about him. Let him be the one to do that if he chooses. He has told you things in confidence and will not appreciate you breaking that trust. It is up to him whether or not he chooses to share such things with others, but you don't have the right to do so without his permission. Be his cheerleader, not his adversary.

On the flip side, singing your man's praises in front of other people will make him feel like your hero. It can be as simple as telling your dinner guest how hard your partner worked on cooking the meat just perfectly and what an amazing cook he is.

Another way that this loyalty thing can go very wrong is something that is all too common. Let's say you had an argument with your boyfriend, and he just won't see your point of view. Later, you go out with your girlfriend, Sasha, tell her all about the argument and of course, she is on your side. Feeling vindicated, you return home and tell your boyfriend that Sasha agrees with you about the issue. This may seem innocent enough; however, your man may interpret it as if you are gathering an army against him. He can't win.

And the next time he sees Sasha, he will feel like she's judging him. The best thing to remember is that you are on the same team as your partner. He isn't your enemy and doesn't need to be vanquished.

4. The need to be close emotionally

Believe it or not, men actually have a strong need and desire for intimacy. We all do as human beings. It just isn't as easy for them to admit because society doesn't foster this as a strong, powerful, manly characteristic. In addition, because of the wiring in their brains, it doesn't come out the same as a feminine-brained person.

Think of it as your feminine gift to make space for the masculine to go deep and be in touch with their emotions. He often needs you to pave the way for him to access these deeper emotions in himself.

One thing to also remember is, as your man begins to trust you, he will begin to reveal more and more of himself. The worst thing you can do is to be critical or judgmental of the things he begins to reveal or he will begin to censor himself around you.

7

Dating 101

What is your dating mindset?

Are you walking around in the world, wishing someone would find you attractive, ask you out and pick you to be their one and only? When you are on a date, are you hoping that you make a good impression on him and that you seem smart enough, fun enough and pretty enough? If so, then your mindset around dating needs some adjustment. You are putting yourself in a position that is bound to make you feel self-conscious. Also, this mindset is the exact opposite of what a man needs in order to find you attractive.

Biologically, men are designed to be the pursuers, and they need to feel like they have been chosen by the woman they desire. They secretly want to win you over. A man wants to prove that he is the man for you. If YOU pick HIM, he feels like he's won you and will stay attracted to you. When a woman is too concerned about whether he likes her or not, it is a turn-off and doesn't instill in his psyche that you are a prize. That said, the best mindset is that YOU are the chooser, not the choos-ee. Imagine what it will feel like when you are dating and open to meeting men but have the experience that you are waiting to see if someone is a good fit for YOU. You aren't worried if they will pick you; you are wondering if you should pick them.

Imagine what it would feel like to go on a date with the knowledge that you are amazing and don't have to prove anything. Imagine being on this date feeling relaxed and confident, curious about this person in front of you and getting a sense whether or not he would be a man YOU would want in your life.

Not only does this give more power back to you, it actually helps create the right foundation for your budding relationship. What's more, it boosts your sense of confidence. If you already know that you are an amazing catch (which comes back to those pesky beliefs we talked about) then you are well aware that any man would be lucky to be chosen by you. Be the chooser.

Men Date Better Than Women

Men tend to have a better frame around dating than women do. Women are often looking for their soul mates, their future husbands, and/or the fathers of their future children. They have a lot wrapped up in dating and meeting people. This search often causes them to future trip and to miss red flags. It puts a lot of pressure on this stranger in front of you when you are already walking down the aisle in your mind, even before the second date.

I will tell you a little secret about men. They are not looking for their soul mates. They are not searching for their future wives or the mothers of their children or even looking for girlfriends. I am not saying they don't want these things, but they are usually not focused on them. What a man tends to look for is a woman he finds attractive who he can go on one date with. If that date goes well then he would like another date and so forth. He begins to think about commitment, marriage and such after he feels like the person he is with is a good fit for that next step, not before. In the beginning of a dating relationship, this is a much better mindset then future tripping. It will keep you clear and focused on the present, and if things don't work out, you don't have to mourn the loss of the marriage and family that you had made up in your mind. It keeps it lighter, with less pressure and a lot more fun. If you can keep things lighthearted in the beginning, not only will dating be more fun and less pressure, but you will be able to pay attention to how you are really feeling with this person. When you stay in the present, you can tune into your compass much more easily.

Flirting

Definition: *To act amorously and to show attraction without serious intent. To play at love.*

I love the definition "to play at love." Playfulness and lightheartedness is a very nice way to approach love and attraction. When we become too serious about anything, it becomes too important. When things are too important then they have a built-in feature of failure or success. What if dating was all just play?

There is a lot that goes into good flirting, and some people are naturals at it. Some people are over the top with their advances, and they come on so strongly that they turn people off. On the other hand, some have their signaling radars set at such a low frequency that no one can ever tell if they are attracted to anyone. These are the people who go out and don't do anything to engage with others and then get frustrated that no one approaches them. Still, others have the intensity switch set just right, where they can subtly let people know they are interested without scaring them off. Don't worry, even if being a flirt isn't your most comfortable realm, I will teach you an easy tip that anyone can do, and that most people don't do enough of that will help.

We are way more in tune with other humans then we think. We are designed to pick up certain clues from people to determine whether or not they are interested, approachable or dangerous. We scan body language and facial cues without even realizing that we are doing it. Our reptilian brain is always scanning to see whether someone is safe or not. How does it know if someone is open or closed or safe to talk to?

There is a lot that goes into the study of body language and what it means that we won't go into, but as I promised, I will tell you the number one, sure-fire trick to let someone know that you are open and not going to hurt him.

SMILE!

Yup, that's it. Super simple, yet most of the time we are not doing it enough or when it counts the most. In fact, quite often when we are interested in someone, we start to feel nervous and tense —all of which shows up on our faces. We might look blank, tight-lipped and intense when we are nervous. This signals to others that we are not approachable, nor are we friendly. This is the opposite of what we would like to communicate when we are attracted to someone or when we are out hoping to meet men for dating.

Flirting redefined

As I mentioned, it is best for a man to pursue a woman so he can feel like he is winning her over. But think about this: A man who wants to approach a woman who he is attracted to has a 50/50 chance of being rejected. Being rejected is also one of the biggest universal fears. Most everyone who has social anxiety can attest to the fact that the biggest fear is one of not being accepted, thus rejected. Because of this, if he can't read you or tell if you are open to him, most likely he will not approach you. However, if you look over at him and smile, you are sending a very clear message. It is the human equivalent of a dog wagging its tail to show that it is friendly.

Speaking of, I used to have a miniature schnauzer whose tail was docked too short. So when she approached other dogs, she was unable to signal to them that she was friendly. The other dogs often picked fights with her because she couldn't adequately communicate her intentions. The same is true with smiling. Here is the scene: You are at a party or event and you spot a cute guy. What is the first thing your average woman does when he catches their eye?

Most of the time she will quickly look away and avoid eye contact as much as possible because she is nervous. What message do you think this sends to said hottie?

And you wonder why no one who you find attractive ever approaches you and why it is that you go home sad and frustrated.

Here is a different scenario: you spot a cutie and catch his eye. You smile and hold his gaze for about three seconds and then look away. A few minutes later, catch his eye again and smile again before looking away. This tells him is that you are open to him approaching you. The chances of him being rejected go way down, which most likely will give him the courage to come up to you.

Think of flirting as inviting a man to interact with you. He is the pursuer and the choos-ee. You are the pursued and the chooser. Simple, right? Now, if you are truly "playing at love," then even if he doesn't approach, it is all just play. I know, it seems scary at first to just smile at strangers, especially if you live in an urban environment or in certain parts of the world where we are conditioned to keep our heads down, not to make eye contact with people and not to smile at strangers. Trust yourself to know who to give the "open for approach" signals to and who not to. If you are not in the habit of smiling at strangers or if the thought of doing it terrifies you, you are not alone. But it really is going to make meeting a good man much easier and quicker. The best thing to do is just practice smiling at people who you might not be attracted to, so your system gets used to it when the stakes aren't as high. Practice smiling at your barista, the grocery clerk, your neighbor, you name it. With practice, you will begin to feel safer and more comfortable doing it. So then when Mr. Cutie Pants crosses your path, it won't be such a stretch. You will just be that person who smiles at strangers.

8

Stages of Relationship
"From Dating to Commitment"

From casual to commitment

I f you want to go from a casual thing to a commitment with the man you are seeing, there are a few things to remember that will make your journey easier.

First, make sure he is a man with whom you really want to be in a committed relationship. As always, it is important to refer to your list and compass of how you want to "feel" with your partner and to adhere to the bottom line that you wrote down earlier. It will take some time to get to know someone so don't rule people out too quickly, but if any of your red flags or non-negotiable behaviors come up, do yourself a favor and get out fast!

Remember, YOU are the one choosing the best partner for you. Be mindful if you start to feel like you need to prove yourself to him or are trying to win him over. These feelings are just those old limiting beliefs, pulling you into negative thinking, telling you that you aren't enough and that you need to prove your worthiness. To the best of your ability, sit in the reality that you are already lovable and good enough and that there is NOTHING you need to do to prove that to anyone. This is a much more powerful place to be when choosing a partner.

There are, however, some things you should be paying attention to early on in your own behavior. These things will set the stage for your relationship to move to a more committed place rather than stalling out in casual land.

A man begins to warm up to the idea of a woman being in his life when he recognizes three important things about her:

1. She is picky.

When he sees that you expect him to have his life together emotionally, socially and financially as a requirement to be with you, it shows him that you don't spend time with just anyone. Remember, a man wants to feel special. Being picky is good. If you don't get into relationships with just anyone, then he will want to rise to the occasion and be your special guy. If you are picky, you start to be seen as more of a prize and a higher status women.

Women have been known to lower their standards just so they can be in a relationship. This rarely works out. The men they end up with will always disappoint them in the end. A man is rarely motivated to better himself for a woman. Loving someone for where they are in life is great but be aware that falling in love with potential will most likely end in heartache and struggle. If you are completely content with where your man is emotionally, socially and financially, and you're okay with the way he handles his responsibilities in life, then go for it. But if it bothers you in any way, make sure you let him know early on in a kind way, even by just stating what you are really looking for in a relationship. If he wants to be with you, he will know where your boundaries are and adhere to them and want to make you happy. If he knows where you stand and he doesn't adjust, then he probably can't because of his own emotional limitations, or he just doesn't want to.

Although you should always be using your compass to gauge every budding relationship, sometimes a man might be fine with adjusting something if it works better for you. But you will never know until you say something.

For instance, let's say he is thirty minutes late meeting you and doesn't really have an explanation, nor did he let you know he was running late. Maybe he is consistently late with most of his engagements. Instead of getting upset about it, you can clearly be happy to see him when he arrives and then calmly say, "I was waiting for you. Next time, if you are running late, will you let me know?" Or, you can say, "I understand that things happen, but I am a punctual person, and I really love it when other people are on time as well." Saying this with a pleasant voice won't put him on the defensive but it will let him know that you're not afraid to speak up when things aren't working. On that note, there is a way to communicate your standards in a way that doesn't shut him down. We will discuss that later in the "Asking for What You Want" chapter.

2. Don't be his sex buddy

You are a woman who won't stand for just a purely physical relationship. Please know that men and women see sex differently. A man can have sex without experiencing ANY desire for a relationship, so don't assume that just because you're having sex, that he is thinking that you are in a relationship. Don't stand for him calling you up just to invite you over for sex. If he isn't pursuing you to win you over, you have already lost. I mean that if he isn't dating you, trying to get to know you and planning dates, then he is just sleeping with you. You won't be able to change the way he sees you if you have already fallen into this category, so it is best to just walk away. Unless, of course, you are fine with just a purely physical relationship and nothing more.

In the early stages of getting to know someone, a good way to avoid being put into the "casual sex girl" category is to not sleep with him right away. I am not saying this as a way to be prudish or manipulative, but if you have sex with someone right away, you are not giving him a chance to show you who he really is. You don't know if he is worthy of your time and your energy or of your body. He isn't getting a chance to win you over. I am not saying that sex is a prize that you give someone for good behavior but it is a bonding activity. Women tend to get more attached by being sexual than men do. So be certain that this person is really someone who fits your compass and is showing you that he thinks highly enough of you that he doesn't require sex from you to stick around.

3. Know that men move slower

One of the bigger complaints that I hear from women is that they don't know how their new love interests feel about them or if they want a committed relationship or not.

A man's commitment speed is often slower than a woman's. Most men aren't out there looking for a relationship just for the sake of having one. Instead, they meet a woman and decide if they want to have a relationship with HER in particular, knowing this will and should take time. Some women, on the other hand, are on a mission to create a relationship and sometimes this desire can lead them to choose men who are not necessarily a good fit because their desire for a relationship clouds their judgment.

Men take longer to decide if they want a relationship with a woman because they are trying her on in their lives first. A man will wait to see what life might be like with a woman he is interested in before he makes that commitment. By the way, even though it might seem like men in general are commitment-phobes, I personally agree with waiting to see if someone is a good fit before jumping into something deeper. In the beginning stages, you should be a "no" or a "maybe" about someone. There is no way to tell if someone is a "yes" until you have spent enough time with him and tried him on in your life. Don't let your desires and fantasies of love get the better of you here.

To build a solid foundation for a healthy relationship, there will be different stages that your dating life with someone will need to go through before you end up in a committed partnership. Every stage is a necessary part of creating a solid and stable relationship. If one of the stages is skipped, it can cause weakness or a crack in the foundation. There are specific things that need to happen in each stage to move it forward and there are also behaviors that might throw the whole process off without you even knowing it.

Working with my clients over the years, I have seen many relationships begin and end. I have seen a pattern in each beginning and ending. I have noticed that there is a timetable to get to commitment, and that during each stage, things can go right to move it to the next stage and things can often go wrong and cause the budding relationship to stop cold. There are three specific stages that consist of two- to three-month time frames. Because of this, I have named the stages of dating from casual to commitment, *trimesters*.

Just as in pregnancy, each trimester feels different, and each trimester is important for developing different parts of the new life. Each dating trimester is important for building and strengthening parts of the budding relationship.

Please know that these time frames are just a rough estimate, based on the countless relationships I have observed, and that the timing is not set in stone. Every experience is unique.

First Trimester-the attraction stage

The first trimester of dating is called the attraction stage. This is the beginning stage of dating someone. You meet. You feel attracted. You begin spending more time with each other. You may feel giddy, you may feel the elation of the newness and you may feel the chemical rush of dopamine and serotonin in your system. You feel attracted to this person, which makes you want to spend more time with him. There are butterflies in your stomach when you think about him. There is the zing in your body when your phone rings. Your mind wanders and thoughts of him fill your mind. These are all biological responses that ensure mating and the continuation of the species. It is a normal part of being human. It is exhilarating and can be a fun part of dating, HOWEVER, these biological feelings can also cloud your clear vision of who this person really is.

There are a few things to remember that will help move this stage forward in a good way, and there are also some pitfalls to look out for. Certain things can happen in this stage that might end things quickly or create an unsteady foundation.

Men look at life as if they are winning or they are losing

Deep down, what is mostly organizing a man's motivation or vision is a virtual voice inside his head that is subconsciously asking, "Am I winning or am I losing?" A man wants to win. Winning to his psyche means that he is successful in life. His sense of being a man is wrapped up in whether or not he is successful. This is good to know because not only is he looking at everything in his life in terms of winning or losing, but everything in his life is also a problem to solve. Make no mistake: you will be a problem to solve. Your relationship will be a problem to solve as well as his career and whatever else he is focused on. If he can't win at what he is focusing on, he will eventually stop working toward it. When it comes to dating, this is what it boils down to: if he can't win at making you happy or being seen as a successful partner, he will eventually shut down and leave. How will you help him win or inadvertently make him lose and fail?

She won't receive the gifts he is giving

One big thing that will throw off the progress of the first trimester is when a woman has a weak receiving muscle. The best thing that can happen in the first trimester is that he gives to her and does nice things for her and she receives what he is offering. Whether they are compliments, dinners or gestures such as opening the door for you, all of these are gifts he's bestowing to show you that he can take care of you and win you over. If you have a hard time receiving, then this might throw everything off. Remember, a man needs to win and he does so by giving and making you happy. If you cannot receive, then he cannot win, and he will move on to a different situation where he can.

Terry had such low self-esteem that it was difficult for her to even receive compliments without throwing them back at the giver by dismissing them. She called me one night as she was getting ready for the first date with a man from work she had felt a connection with. She was nervous. He wanted to meet her at an expensive wine bar. She told me that she was planning on getting there thirty minutes early so she would be able to buy her own glass of wine. She hated the thought of him buying her something. I managed to convince her to let him buy her a glass of wine. I told her that a man never does anything he doesn't want to do. So, if he offers, it is because he wants to and it will make him happy to give to her. He was the one who picked the spot. He probably imagined that she would be impressed by its quaintness. He wanted to plan a nice evening for her. If she wouldn't let him succeed at this, then any potential romantic connection between them was already dead in the water. She later reported that she forced herself to receive without hesitation that night, and at the end of the night when thanking him for such a thoughtful, fun evening, she saw a smile on his face that indicated that he felt appreciated. He looked satisfied. He was beaming, and he quickly asked her out again for the following week.

Being able to properly receive is imperative for a healthy relationship. Think of it like this: Let's say you found an amazing birthday present for your best friend. You bought it and wrapped it up. The day came and you were so excited to see her face when she opened your gift. You went over to her house and handed her present, anticipating her delight. Then she quietly handed it back to you without even opening it saying, "No thank you. I'm not taking gifts for my birthday this year." How would you feel? You would most likely feel crushed. You were looking forward to the act of giving. You were looking forward to making your friend happy. You weren't expecting anything in return; her happiness would be your gift. This is the exact same concept I am speaking about when it comes to dating men. If you refuse his gifts, it is as crushing as the above birthday scenario. When you receive his gifts, your happiness and gratitude are all he needs in return to know that he was of value in your life.

There are many reasons why a woman might feel awkward about fully receiving. If she has low self-esteem and limiting beliefs about her worthiness, it will feel uncomfortable when someone wants to give to her. If she feels that receiving means she is giving up control and it leaves her feeling powerless when she surrenders, then she will always resist the care a man has to offer her.

She future trips

Now is a gift; that is why they call it the present. Ha. All kidding aside, future tripping in the first trimester is a recipe for disaster. This is the "get to know you stage." If you are interested in someone, it is easy to fall into the trap of fantasizing about your wedding, about the trips you will take, what it will be like when you live together and what your parents will think of him. It is fun to fantasize about these things and it is also very dangerous. Future tripping like this will cause you to become more attached to him then you should be at this stage of the game. You aren't really seeing the real him either. You become attached to your projection of him and who you want him to be rather than who he is. You might become so attached to your fantasy that you begin to miss red flags. You are walking down the aisle before you have even had your second date. If things don't work out, you will have a lot more to mourn. Instead of just saying, "Oh well that wasn't a good fit," you will have to mourn your fantasy marriage, and all the wonderful times you spent with him in your head. It is best to stay in the present. Ask yourself, "Who is this person in front of me?" "How do I feel right now when I am with him?" Go back to your compass. Make sure you are really seeing who is in front of you and not just your made-up desires.

She pursues him

Because a man's relationship speed might be slower than a woman's, she may get impatient and want to push the relationship forward faster than it is going. We might see her asking him out, doing more of the planning in the dating stage, calling more and just generally making herself very available and valuable to him. This might work in the beginning; however, in order to keep his attraction and attention, she needs to let him pursue and win her over.

In the first trimester, it is important for the masculine to win over the feminine. The masculine brain is wired to prove his usefulness to the opposite sex. And remember: the masculine brain wants to win you over. He wants to make you happy. When you are happy he wins. He wants to be chosen by you, since that means he wins. When he wins, he is motivated to keep winning. If a woman is doing the pursuing, then there is nothing to win. It doesn't become that intriguing to a man's system when there is no challenge or problem to solve. It isn't true winning when someone just throws you the race. I am not suggesting playing games or playing hard to get. What I am saying is sit back, relax and let him win.

In order for a man to commit to a long relationship, he needs to feel like he can be useful and make a woman happy. If he cannot prove that to himself by doing nice things for her that are warmly received, he won't get the confirmation that he needs to feel happy or secure in the relationship. If she is pursuing, he will never know if he has won her over.

Just like with a pregnancy, you don't know for certain if it is viable until after the first three months. Take it slow. Have fun. You don't know if he is Mr. Right until you spend enough time with him. Just keep checking in with your emotional compass.

Second Trimester- the uncertainty stage

Things have been going great. You are spending more time with this person. You are feeling closer to him. You are getting more comfortable around him and then BAM! He disappears. You have hit the "uncertainty stage." This will come at some point. It has different ways that it shows up and can last for a day up until about a month or so. On your end, it could look like you start to get cold feet. You might start to question some of his behaviors or get picky about things that didn't seem to bother you before. It can also show up when he pulls away and disappears.

The man who was actively pursuing you now seems to be missing in action. He isn't getting back to you. He isn't asking you out as much. Often this happens just after you spent an incredible weekend away together or after you have met his parents. It will tend to happen about two or three months into dating someone regularly. Women are so caught off guard when this happens, and it can feel awful. The uncertainty stage sucks AND it is also a very necessary part of building a foundation. Both parties at this point need to pull back and assess whether they want to continue into a more committed situation. It is good to actually review what has been taking place and choose instead of just ending up in something just because it was happening and you didn't think about it. Don't you want to be with someone you have really chosen and who has consciously chosen you?

Remember how the masculine brain processes emotions? Men need to take a break and pull away to decide how they feel. He can't be in it and decide or even know how he feels until he is away from you. This is why quite often when things are about to move into a different stage, a man will pull away, disappear and go into his cave to make this very important decision. Men are more instinctual in relationships then women tend to be. They might not even be aware that they are pulling away to make a decision. It just feels like a natural thing to do. This has got to be the most frustrating and unpleasant stage of dating. It causes a whole slew of emotions: anxiety, insecurity, anger, sadness and yes, uncertainty.

What is he doing in his cave?

When a man pulls away at this stage, he is asking himself some important questions designed to determine whether he should move the relationship forward or not. He might not even know he is asking these questions, but he is in his cave to figure out how he is doing with you. He is asking himself, "Can I make this woman happy?" This can also be read as, "Am I winning?"

He will use all of the interactions that he had with you in that first trimester to find out the answer to this very important question. Did you let him pursue you? Did you let him make you happy? Could he please you? Basically, he is asking himself if he is a good fit for you. While he is asking himself if he is the right man for you, you should be asking yourself the very same question.

Pitfalls of the second trimester

It is tempting to bang on the door of the man cave and demand some answers. Most likely he hasn't given you any warning that he is taking leave, and how rude of him to not tell you what he is up to! If your guy has actually had the emotional presence to explain to you that he needs some time to feel out the relationship and decide if he is a good fit for you so he can take it to the next level, then you are one lucky woman. Most men will not tell you they are taking a break. They will just vanish. It isn't that they are purposely being rude. Sometimes they don't know the reasons why they feel things; they just feel them or sense them and take action. Pulling away is a natural instinct so he can assess the situation. The worst thing you can do is pound on the door of the man cave and demand some answers.

Give him space. Go live your juicy life. Hopefully, you are dating some other folks, and if so, go spend time with them. Don't sweat it. I know that this is easier said than done. But the more anxious you are about it, the farther you will push him away and the longer it will take him to process and come out. The kicker is, if you get anxious or upset about him pulling away, he begins to feel like he is losing, and he might make a decision based on that feeling.

Let him miss you. A man needs to miss a woman to know that he is into her. Don't chase after him when he disappears. Give him an opportunity to miss you.

Don't give him space as a way to play games. Give him space because you are not the kind of high-quality woman who chases men. You have your own beautiful life and activities and you don't need him to give you any confirmation that you are amazing.

If you have been good about not pursuing him up until this point, you might feel the pull to start pursuing him at this stage. When he pulls away you might feel panicky and then call him more for reassurance. You might push and make more plans with him to ease your mind. All of these behaviors will backfire and make this stage last longer. Also, if he feels that you are being insecure and more demanding in this phase, he might begin to feel that he won't ever be able to have his own space with you if you end up in a serious relationship.

This might sound like I think men are unconscious jerks who women need to handle with kid gloves. This isn't what I am saying. I am saying that men and women are different when it comes to how they decide whether or not they want to be in a relationship. It is helpful for you to know that a man has pulled away because he was beginning to have feelings for you. It began to get deep for him, so he needed time to make sure it was a good fit before moving forward. In a way, this is a pretty respectful thing to do. However, it would be easier if he would just say what he was doing. Or rather, it would be easier if he knew why and what he was doing so he could communicate it accurately.

Don't pursue. Just lean back. Let him come to you when he is done in there. Like I said, in the meantime, go live your juicy life! You can't force him to want to be with you anyway and why would you want to force someone into a relationship? Use this time to see if you really miss HIM. As long as you don't make his pulling away mean anything about you, then you should be able to use this time wisely and really decide if he is a good fit for you. You have had about three months with him and now really is the only time that you have had enough data to make a decision based on facts and not your fantasies.

It will make it easier on you if you remember that he is asking himself if HE is a good fit for you, if HE can make YOU happy, not the other way around. He isn't evaluating you, he is evaluating his capacity for success with you. Winning.

When Jessi came to see me for advice about the man she had recently started dating, she was clearly upset and didn't know what to do. Jessi started dating Mike two months prior, and things were going very well, until last week. She reported that Mike was very romantic and attentive in the beginning. He texted her every day and brought her flowers often. He was eager to move things forward with her and wasn't afraid to tell her how he felt about her. Because Jessi had been through the F.L.I.R.T Courses, she knew that taking it slow in the beginning phase was a good idea, so she often encouraged Mike to slow down so they could take their time getting to know each other. He reluctantly complied. Jessi was convinced that they might not even hit the issues of the second trimester of dating, and eventually, after enough time getting to know each other, they would slide right into a committed relationship.

Jessi reported that the week prior, her mother had been visiting from out of town and Mike was pushing to meet her mom. Jessi knew that it was too soon in their courtship to take it to that level but she agreed anyway. Two days after meeting her mother, Mike sent her a message asking if they could speak on the phone. They rarely talked on the phone, and Jessi was curious as to what was so important to have an arranged phone call. She called him that evening. This is what Mike asked her: "Are we still allowed to date other people?" Jessi was a bit shocked. She had thought they were progressing into more of a commitment but knew that they needed some more time to get to know each other. She had been trying to slow things down so they could build a solid foundation, but this seemed to come out of the blue. She responded, "I guess so, since we are not in an official relationship yet. Why are you asking?" He said, "Well, I met someone and I am curious to see where it goes." Jessi's heart sank. But all she could do was thank him for telling her. The next day, she and Mike met up, and he confessed that he had had sex with that woman the night before, right after they spoke. Jessi was crushed. She had no idea Mike would move so quickly and that she might lose him. She was so upset she left the bar crying. Until then, she had no idea how much she truly felt for him.

She sat in front of me with tears welled up in her eyes. "I don't know what to do," she confessed. "I really want to be with him, but I don't think I can hang with him being with other women." At that moment, it dawned on me what was happening. This WAS a form of second trimester uncertainty. Mike had been getting closer and closer to Jessi, and his version of pulling away or going into the cave was to bring another woman into the mix. When I explained this to her, she seemed relieved. She still wasn't comfortable with him being with other women, but now she knew what was happening and how to proceed. She decided to call Mike up and explain how she felt. She said although it made her uncomfortable, she couldn't tell him not to date other people because they were not in a relationship, and she didn't know for sure if that was what she was ready for. She told *him that she had been enjoying getting to know him and that so far it seemed like they might be a good fit, but she just wasn't sure. Because of this uncertainty, she was going to have to be ok with him dating other people, but there might come a day when she wasn't ok with it anymore and she would have to walk away. Saying this to him made her feel more powerful and in control. She realized that she was the one who wasn't ready because she was still deciding if he was a good fit for her, not the other way around.*

Three weeks passed and then she got a message from Mike, saying he was finished with dating other people and he wanted to end it with the other woman. He wanted to focus all of his energy on Jessi. He knew for certain now that he had other experiences to compare it to. Yes, second trimester. Mike needed the other experiences to really feel what Jessi meant to him. Because Jessi gave him space and didn't promise to stick around or chase him, he came to her out of his own choice. She didn't say yes right away, though. She asked if they could sit down and compare some notes about what they both really wanted in a relationship to make sure they were on the same page. They did, and they have been happy together now for a year with much more to come. They both chose each other and went into it very consciously, and they are committed to creating a healthy foundation for their love to flourish.

Third Trimester: we are in a relationship

Once you have gone through your compass list and assessed what went on in the first trimester, and once he comes out of the cave, you will need to decide: "Is this where I want to spend my time and energy? Is this relationship giving me what I want? Do I like spending time with this person? Do I see us having a healthy future together?" If the answer is "yes" for both of you then it is time to have a discussion.

The "Where do you want to go from here?" conversation. The "Are we in a relationship?" conversation. You are in a relationship only after you have a discussion about it. Many a woman has made the mistake of assuming that a man was her boyfriend simply because they were spending time together, and has often been crushed to eventually find out that the person she was with did not feel the same way.

During this relationship conversation, it is a good idea to discuss what both of your relationship requirements are. Monogamy? How many days or nights a week would you like to spend together? How much alone time does each of you need? This kind of detailed discussion will cut down on the potential for any miscommunication and expectations not being fulfilled. Remember this is a negotiation. It isn't the law. You both need to be happy and fulfilled in order for it to work.

Once you are in a relationship, your neurology might begin to relax. You finally know what is happening and you might begin to feel a bit more secure. This is a good thing. You are now able to start creating an even deeper bond with this person now that you know it is serious. However, be careful. This isn't the finish line as you might think. It is the beginning of a new phase and it needs special attention to make sure it keeps going.

Here are some very important things to pay attention to in this stage:

Don't get too comfortable

I know this sounds strange. We all want to feel comfortable around the person we are in a relationship with. You will become to feel more at ease, and this is a good thing. Up to now, you were both showing your best sides. You were out to impress each other and you were curious about each other. The worst thing I see when I am working with married couples is that they take each other for granted and both end up feeling resentful and unappreciated.

Keep taking pride in your appearance. He will appreciate it just as you will when he continues to take care of his own looks for you.

All the little things that your man was doing for you to care for you in the first trimester become normalized, and often women no longer show appreciation for these things. For example, let's say he used to take the garbage out for you when he came to visit. In the beginning, you were probably very thankful. If he is still doing that for you now that he is your boyfriend, please remember to still be thankful and let him know how much it means to you. If he takes you out somewhere, show him you are happy. Keep letting him make plans and do things to make you happy. At this stage, you might start to plan more dates and events and start to pay for some dinners here and there. But don't fully take over. Let him keep winning.

Men think they have won and stop trying

I hear many women complain that once they ended up in a relationship, all the romantic things their guys were doing just stopped. They often feel duped, as if it was a bait and switch situation somehow. As I mentioned, men look at the world and everything that they are doing as if they are winning or they are losing. Dating you was a race and now that he feels like he won, he can sit back and work on another challenge to solve. This sucks! All that juicy romance and the dates he was planning were some of the reasons why you chose him, right? All hope is not lost, however. You just need to gently remind him that the race is not over. He will actually appreciate having to continue to put in the effort with you, because, frankly, he'll get to keep winning! If he has traded in romantic strolls through the park and wine country excursions for staying home to watch yet another episode of the latest TV series on the couch, don't worry. There is a way to fire up his engines again. A simple, "I love it when you plan dates for us. It makes me feel so special and happy," will often do the trick. Then when he does take you out, really make sure he sees you happy and joyful. Let him make you happy. Make sure he knows you appreciate his effort, and he will keep wanting to do it.

Women tend to get controlling and express disappointment in this stage. Newsflash: that doesn't make him want to keep trying with you. It makes him want to quit. So if he takes you out to a movie—even if it is a movie you didn't like—make sure you let him know how happy you were that he planned something and how nice it was to spend time with him out of the house. You don't have to lie and say you loved the movie. Focus on the parts of the date you did love. For more ideas on how to communicate your needs and desires, see the chapter on communicating so he will want to make you happy.

Keep getting to know each other

This is the time to go even deeper with each other. In the beginning, you were probably very curious about every last detail as you tried to figure out who this person was. You probably asked him questions. You were present, listening and genuinely curious. We all love to feel listened to. It feels great when someone wants to know who we are. Just because you are now in a relationship doesn't mean you already know your man fully. In fact, we as humans are constantly growing and changing. You will need to continually get to know someone. The worst thing you can do for intimacy is to stop really seeing and discovering your partner.

I see this in married couples all the time: they think they know their partners and forget to keep getting to know them. Even couples who have been together for only two or three years have probably gone through some changes. It is hurtful to stop wanting to learn more about one another. All the deeper questions you learned in the previous chapter should still be in play in your committed relationship. How do you feel about this and that? Those kinds of questions keep the emotional intimacy alive.

The love chemicals will burn out

During this stage, the high dopamine and serotonin chemicals will level out. When those chemicals are running high, people have a tendency to overlook negative things. Those feel-good chemicals cast a positive filter on most things. That is why people who are "falling in love" have a glow about them. If they're the sort of people who get really stressed and grumpy about things, you might notice they're letting those same annoying things slide with a shrug now that the love chemicals are running throughout their system. In the third trimester, the chemicals will even out. This is a good thing. It is almost impossible to get things done when you are distracted by all of these powerful feelings for someone. But because the chemical levels drop, you might begin to see things that your partner does that you didn't notice before. Or maybe the idiosyncrasies you thought were cute before now begin to bother you. You might start to argue and bicker at this stage. It can be quite a crash down from the euphoric feeling that you had in the first trimester. You might even start to question whether or not you made a good decision in choosing to be with this person because of the crash. I caution you to not jump to such conclusions. Don't worry if you argue. It is normal. Couples will have disagreements and challenges. It is how you work through them that matters. What matters is IF you can resolve issues completely so they don't keep cropping up. In the following chapters, we will discuss communication and getting your needs met.

How couples deal with conflict will either create a stronger bond of trust and connection or it will slowly eat away at any good feelings they might have had for one another. Conflict happens. How you deal with it is your choice, and will make or break the quality of your relationship.

9

Creating a Healthy Relationship that Lasts

Creating a healthy relationship

Now that you have found a relationship, the next big question is how to make it last. How can you create healthy patterns inside of your relationship that are good for you both? How do you establish a foundation that will help your relationship last?

This is sometimes an even harder quest than finding a love interest in the first place. The foundation of a relationship is set up from the beginning, so even if you haven't found that special person yet, it will be beneficial to understand how to create a healthy foundation now so that you can be aware of these things right from the start. Pre-emptive planning is easier to do than fixing something that breaks.

I see many couples in trouble in my office. When they finally come to me for help, often there has been so much damage already done to their bond that it takes a lot of hard work and effort to repair it. Once negative patterns of behavior get started in a relationship, it is difficult to break them, so why not start out with something that will be beneficial in the long term right away? There are some definite elements that create a healthy, joyful bond and some that will destroy it or make it so it is shaky and not secure.

Understanding, generosity and forgiveness

Generosity, understanding and forgiveness are the most powerful gifts to bring to a relationship. Being generous without keeping score, understanding that your partner is human and will make mistakes, and being able to really, truly forgive and let it go, are all the things that lasting, loving relationships have in common.

That being said, these traits must maintain a delicate balance. Giving love, attention and care freely because it comes naturally is the juice for a loving relationship. But how can you give generously and not keep score while still making sure you are not over-giving? It is a subtle distinction that makes a huge difference. If you are giving just to give and not to get love or a sense of appreciation back, then you're on the right track. That sort of mindset is the first indication that you are properly giving, regardless of what comes back. But then how can you tell if you are being taken advantage of by your partner?

In healthy relationships, you will not be able to distinguish who is giving and who is taking. It feels like an even flow between them. It is like a dance. You will be able to trust your gut when it feels like maybe your partner is taking advantage of you or not participating in the giving/receiving dance with you. First and foremost, keep track of your own intentions for your generosity, and that should keep you on track.

Accepting someone as they are

The thing that kills most relationships, destroys trust and diminishes attraction is when you don't feel good enough, or if it feels like your partner wants you to be someone different than who you are. There is a cliché that goes like this: "Men marry women in hopes they never change. Women marry men in hopes that they will."

I have seen an occasional couple where the man is hard on the woman and wants her to be something she is not. But quite often, it is women who come into my office wanting their male partners to be different.

By now, you should understand the significance of using your compass to pick a good partner for you and to keep from being blinded by your desire for a relationship, ignoring red flags and such. Every partner you pick should have an imaginary *As Is* sticker on them. You can't bully, manipulate, or force anyone to be different from who he really is. If you keep that in mind, you will most likely pick a partner who is already a good fit for you or at least good enough. I say good enough because in reality, no one will ever be perfect. There will always be something that you would prefer he had—or didn't have—or behavior that annoys you, but you need to ask yourself if it is a deal breaker. If it is, then don't even continue your dating process with that person because it will never change, and if he does change it, it won't change because of you. If you can live with it, then make a commitment to him (silently) that you will fully accept it. This full acceptance of him and all that he does will create a harmonious, loving bond. Constant nagging, complaining or manipulation will only destroy any good feelings your partner has about you.

The typical scenario that plays out with couples who come to see me for help is that the woman is frustrated with some behavior or she's not getting what she wants, and the man feels like he can never do anything right. Remember the "Am I winning?" concept with men? When you try to change him, he is already losing, and he will eventually lose interest in you and the relationship. He might try to win and be challenged in a good way by the complaints that you offer him, but the results are only temporary. He will eventually give up and withdraw when he sees that he can't win with you. I am not saying that you aren't allowed to request and ask for your needs and desires to be met but there is a mindset and a way to do it that won't leave your man feeling like he can't win. We will go over the way to communicate to get your needs met in the next chapter.

Forgive and forget

The relationships I see that have lasted for years, where both people are still very much in love, have something at the core that makes this so. If you delve in deep enough when you begin to investigate the secret sauce to long-lasting love, you will find that the ability to forgive is at the core.

Face it: if you are with someone long enough, there is bound to be something that you say or do, or that he says or does, that will be hurtful or make you angry. If you hold onto these grudges even after they've been apologized for, they will become like tiny molecules of resentment and mistrust. Eventually, all these molecules will add up and become how you see your partner all the time. You will come to see him as someone who hurts you, someone who makes you angry and someone you can't trust. Why would you want to be with someone who you feel that way about?

If there has been a violation and an apology, and the two of you have come to an understanding that has happened after a conflict, then you need to let it go and forget it. Please realize that the majority of people do not set out to hurt others intentionally. If you feel like your guy is trying to hurt you on purpose, then you shouldn't be with him anyway.

Everyone should get a clean slate. The way women often communicate, especially if they are upset, doesn't get them the authentic apology they need to get so they can move on and forget. A woman will often attack the man who has upset her in a way that shuts him down and backs him into a corner so he doesn't know how to even apologize without groveling and becoming weak. In the next chapter, we will talk about how to make requests and deal with conflict without damaging the bond.

Is he your friend or your enemy?

If you consider your guy to be a friend or an ally, you will be more forgiving and tolerant of him because you assume that he has your back even if he messes up once in a while. If you view him as your enemy or as someone who doesn't care or is out to get you, then you will assume that he's either indifferent or cruel. With this mindset, you'll react more strongly toward him when he does something upsetting than you would if you considered him a friend, rather than an enemy.

Ask yourself which one your partner is to you. Think about your past relationships. Were they seen as friends? As enemies? Both? You may be surprised to learn that some women, when asked to be honest about this, do feel like their partners are their enemies and not their friends. You can see how this dynamic would play out in creating a combative, non-supportive, hostile relationship. If you keep in mind that your partner is your friend and actually does care, then if he does something by accident to hurt or upset you, you won't automatically assume that he is being malicious.

Unhealthy bonds

Codependency is a word that gets thrown out there a lot. It is a huge topic that I won't go into in depth. Here's a brief explanation: Codependents need other people to like them in order to feel okay about themselves. They're afraid of being rejected or abandoned, even if they can function on their own. In a codependent relationship, there are poor boundaries. It can show up like you being preoccupied with your partner's moods, happiness or their day-to-day activities, so much that you lose your own sense of self. Often people who display codependent behavior have grown up in abusive or neglectful homes where pleasing a parent was the only way they felt they could get love and attention. This goes back to some of the beliefs we talked about earlier. Codependents base their self-worth and lovability on whether or not their partners see them, pay attention to them or continue to be in relationships with them. The opposite of codependency is called differentiation. In short, a well-differentiated sense of self means that your self-worth and sense of value don't rely on what your partner does or what he says or doesn't say or even if he is in a relationship with you or not. Your sense of self is solid and does not depend on others. A person with a well-differentiated self can have boundaries without fearing that she will lose someone or be rejected. She is able to calmly express her needs and desires. She is able to have her own life separate from her partner as well as a shared life without losing a sense of herself.

If you feel like you may have some codependent beliefs or behaviors, I encourage you to read more about codependency to decide for yourself and seek the help that you need. Codependent relationships will never give you what you ultimately want. In fact, they sometimes just deepen the wounds that you might already have from childhood.

Lily couldn't stop obsessing about her boyfriend, Evan. Evan was having a hard time. Having recently lost his job, he was depressed and lost. All Lily could talk about when she was out with her friends was Evan and his problems. She spent all of her free time looking for jobs for him or reading self-help books for him and then trying to get him to swallow the concepts she was reading about. Lily was getting more and more stressed. The more she tried to pull Evan out of his funk and the more she pushed him, the more he dug his heels in and remained stuck. Lily had grown up with a depressed, suicidal mother and spent the majority of her childhood focused on her mom's moods. She tried to be a source of joy for her mom so she wouldn't kill herself. This same panicky energy began to resurface once Evan hit his rut. It sent Lily's subconscious into the same panic she felt as a child. The problem with micromanaging Evan's emotions was that it drove them farther apart. He resisted her help because he didn't want to be treated like he was a child or incompetent. Lily couldn't stand his state because she was terrified of being abandoned. It was a self-fulfilling prophecy as her behavior actually did push him away.

Once she began to look at how invested she was in Evan's life and pulled back a bit, Evan was able to take the steps he needed to help himself. When Lily was in the way, all he could do was shut down more. Lily began to understand and eventually came to terms with the difference in coping mechanisms that she and Evan utilized. In getting comfortable with the differentiation, they were able to have more intimacy and real closeness.

Codependency-fused verses differentiated

Here are some behaviors and thoughts that are considered codependent:

* Trying to please your partner and worrying about what he thinks of you.
* Your self-esteem being dependent on your partner.
* Your self-worth being measured by external validation.
* Acting unconsciously out of childhood trauma or triggers.
* Blaming others or playing the victim and/or being the victim to get attention.
* Needing to always be right or always believing that you are wrong.
* Being dependent on others to soothe you. Not being able to self- soothe.
* Giving with an agenda to get love back.
* Changing who you are to please or control others.
* Rescuing people or overly worrying about them.
* Staying in harmful relationships out of fear of being on your own.

Here are some traits that are considered healthy and differentiated:

Traits of differentiation

* Being able to maintain yourself and your center in a relationship.
* You can say yes, no or maybe.
* Articulating your feelings and being truthful even when bringing up difficult topics.

* Keeping your self-esteem constant and not dependent on the opinions of others.
* Resisting the urge to absorb others' feelings.
* Knowing it is not your responsibility to fix other people's problems.
* Knowing your value is a given no matter what is happening in the relationship.
* Trusting your own internal wisdom instead of relying on others to tell you what to do, think or believe.
* Feeling comfortable and not being threatened by different points of view or beliefs.
* Recognizing signs of manipulation. Trusting wisely not blindly.
* Ability to examine your own intentions and not manipulate others.
* Ability to self-reflect and self-confront.
* Willingness to take responsibility for your actions and can apologize if necessary.
* Ability to leave harmful relationships.
* Ability to ask for and receive support without feeling compromised.
* Giving without an agenda and without feeling like you are giving away too much of yourself.
* Seeing others clearly and getting to know who people are instead of seeing them through your own expectations.
* Ability to comfort and soothe yourself.
* Possessing your own inner resources to take care of your emotions and not demanding that your partner take care of your emotions.

Men won't have sex with their mothers or teachers

Women who have begun to mother or teach the men they are with will undoubtedly be unhappy and unfulfilled in their relationships. If you have found yourself in the role of your man's guide and helper, the sex will most likely fizzle at some point. If you are pulled to take care of him, to mother him, the sex will end even faster. We are programmed as humans to not want to have sex with our mothers or authoritative figures.

I see this so often. A woman who is doing well in her life and on a path of spiritual or personal growth meets a man who doesn't quite have his life together. Maybe he is struggling in his personal development. She jumps in, putting herself into the role of spiritual or life teacher. This dynamic means that you are not his equal and he is not on your level, which will kill the attraction on both sides.

You are your partner's cheerleader, not his coach. You are there to support his efforts but not lead the way. I know you might be saying to yourself right now, "But I don't like where he is with his life." Once again, I will have you refer back to your compass. He has to be acceptable to you "as is." Trying to "fix" him will lead to a huge amount of conflict and heartache for both of you.

On the other hand, it is normal and healthy for both of you to grow and to help each other along the way. You are not here to coddle one another, which can leave you both stagnant and stuck. The difference between helping but not enabling or guiding is subtle but huge. The difference lies in your motivation and intention. Let's say, for example, you see your partner continually wasting time and procrastinating even though he has expressed to you a desire to work on a project that really excites him. If you were trying to be his guide, your internal stance would be: "I have to make him stop procrastinating. Can't he see that he is wasting his life? I can't be with a partner who's living his life this way, so I need to help him change."

If you were in a position of helping rather than enabling, in cheerleader mode rather than teacher mode, your mindset would be quite different. You might want to keep the project fresh in his mind by making an observation to him. "I know you're super excited about that project you told me about. So how is it going?" This puts him back in the driver's seat. He's being responsible for himself, but also gives him a bit of witnessing that is supportive, not pushy. He might even be able to open up to you after that and share his thoughts on the project instead of shutting down and feeling like a little boy who needs to please mommy. Can you see how the latter actually creates more of a bond and doesn't change the power dynamic?

Here are some things that will cause major heartache and an unhealthy bond:

Expecting him to fill you up

We mentioned this earlier. If you need a relationship to make you feel whole, you are putting unreasonable expectations on someone else. Your guy will eventually fail and let you down. If you are with someone in order to feel better about your own life, you are falling into the codependent range. Every time he doesn't do what you want or what you expect, you will not only be disappointed but it has a lot more weight if your happiness depends on him being a certain way. You will most likely end up being more controlling, upset and nagging if this is the case. Your man will eventually pull away because there is too much pressure to be perfect.

Your happiness and a sense of fulfillment should never depend on another person or you will be always at his mercy. Take control and responsibility for your own sense of well-being. Do the things that make you happy. Do what fills you up. Make that your priority and your relationship can then be a cherry on top of something already good.

Bad reasons for wanting a relationship

There are a few bad reasons for wanting a relationship. Your motivation for love will always show through in how and who you pick. Later, after the love chemicals wear off, it will show up in the kind of bond that you have with him. If you have unhealthy reasons for wanting a partner, it will be very difficult to create a healthy relationship. So yes, a healthy love life and partnership begins with you even before you meet your guy. What do you want? What are you trying to gain by having a partner? What drives you to seek out love? Be honest with yourself. All answers are fine, and they may help point you to an area of your thought process in need of some healing or help.

Below are some of the common reasons that don't work very well for being in a relationship.

Wanting a relationship to make you feel secure

Yes, this is a very common motivator for most people. We are pack animals, and we're meant to be in groups. We are not meant to be alone. Life is to be shared, and it is much safer when you have people around to support you. It is natural to want someone in your life you can rely on. However, it gets tricky when people feel desperate about not having that special someone in their lives. In their desperation, they might be less choosey about who they pick. What's more, that desperation will drive people away at the same time. When and if you find this person, who will make your life feel more stable, then all he has to do is not comply or do something that doesn't fit the script, and you go crashing back into insecurity.

When I saw Linda and Bill in my office, they had already separated but were trying to put the pieces back together. Linda was all tears and Bill was stoic. They had been together for fifteen years right out of college. Bill had recently gone through a life crisis, and in a way to pull himself out of his slump, he began to run and train for marathons. He would go running almost every weekend for hours at a time and sometimes during the week. Clearly, he was trying to find some passion in his life. Training was helping him bring back some of the vitality he had lost over the years with his burnout. Linda, however, was upset. Bill was gone a lot, and she was left spending time alone. She felt abandoned. She spoke of his running almost as if it were his mistress. Linda had been a very shy person all through school and had come to rely on Bill as not only her husband and best friend but really as her only friend. When he needed to pull away for his own self-discovery, she fell apart because he was all she had. She was so threatened by this hobby—a healthy hobby that was actually helping Bill out of a depression— that it became the thing that separated them. The problem wasn't the running, of course. It was Linda's control over Bill and the fact that she was so threatened by something he desperately needed. He felt trapped and felt like he had to choose between making Linda happy or making himself happy. It boiled down to an either/or situation, and so he requested a separation to escape the pressure of being her only life vest.

People who feel like they have to negate themselves or their passions in order to appease their partners will eventually leave or become so resentful that it will erode any good feelings between them. If they do not physically leave, they will emotionally shut down parts of themselves to preserve a sense of their own autonomies.

No one should feel completely responsible for the care of another person outside of a parent/child relationship. One person cannot fill all of your needs either. You are much better off having many people in your life that fill different areas. That way you are not only relying on one person for everything and all of your needs.

Wanting a relationship to prove that you are lovable

If you are basing your lovability on whether or not you are in a relationship, you are heading for a rough road ahead. This goes back to the belief chapter in the beginning. If you have healthy self-esteem then you already know you're lovable and worthy even if you are single. Knowing who you truly are and accepting yourself fully is a huge strength. That means you will feel fine about yourself whether you are single, in a relationship, just dating or if your partner breaks up with you. Just because you might still be single and haven't found your match yet has nothing to do with you as a person. It might mean that it isn't the right time yet. It might mean that you are still working on some things that we discussed earlier in the book. It might not mean anything. It might just be down to timing or luck. It doesn't mean that you are broken. It doesn't mean that you're unlovable or that there is anything wrong with you. If you can believe that then you are well on your way to being more empowered in both your relationships and your singlehood.

Gretchen was heartbroken and frantic by the time I met her. At thirty-nine years old, she wanted desperately to find a partner and get married. She'd had many relationships prior but none were a really good fit for the long term. She had given into the societal pressure of not being married yet at her age, and she was crashing hard. On a daily basis, she was looking in the mirror, trying to figure out what might be wrong with her that would explain why she remained single. Was it her looks? Her personality? The fact that she wasn't as financially solid as some of her friends? Was she too weird or off the wall? You see these were not new feelings for Gretchen. She had felt like there was something wrong with since she was a kid. Her parents had been distant, and not very loving or affectionate people. Gretchen grew up feeling alone and unworthy of their love and attention. This dynamic kept playing out in her love relationships as the years went by. When she was in a relationship, the gnawing feelings of not being lovable subsided a bit, but what took its place was an anxious need to make sure her partners would keep loving her. And so she went out of her way to be indispensable to them. Gretchen at her core did not feel lovable just as she was. She had to be or do something to earn love. You can see how this belief was the real reason she felt so awful. Fortunately, once Gretchen started to address the real issues of her childhood, she began to realize she was already lovable and that she didn't need a relationship to prove her worth. Not only did this realization calm her anxieties while she was waiting for Mr. Right, but it also was the reason WHY she met Mr. Right six months later.

Do you want to be Wonder Woman?

Do you have a habit of picking men who need your help in some way? Maybe they are struggling financially, or have failed to launch in some way. Maybe they are having a hard time emotionally. When you meet these types of men, are you drawn to help, heal or save them somehow? If so, you might want to examine this pattern. Often people who pick partners who need them in some way don't feel good enough on their own merit. To ensure that their partners stay with them, they make themselves indispensable in one way or another. A woman might become her man's spiritual teacher, his counselor or his financial advisor.

You can offer yourself up as a problem solver, and a guy might grab on to you and not leave you, but it isn't because he really sees you or loves you. It is because he needs you. A man who can't take care of his own life, his own growth or his own independence will never be what you want in a partner. You will find yourself constantly carrying the load and doing the brunt of the emotional work in the relationship. You will eventually become drained and resentful. Not only that but as I mentioned before, if you put yourself in the role of his guide, the sexual attraction will dwindle. You cannot be your lover's mom or therapist without the feeling of attraction being compromised. We are deeply programmed to not want to have sex with our mom or dads. A man will become emasculated if you are the one telling him how to live his life, how to grow, etc. To put it bluntly, he won't be able to get it up for a woman who he sees as having authority over him.

Are you waiting for your knight in shining armor to save you?

Do you secretly want a man to show up and save you? Save you from your loneliness? From your sadness? From your life? Do you feel broken and believe that once you find your knight, his love will heal you and make it all better? If so, you are in danger of picking a man for the wrong reasons. A man won't save you or make your life that much better. In fact, if you aren't happy now, then you will be even less happy in a relationship. Your happiness will be dependent on whether or not he complies with being your hero. What if he lets you down? The only one who can save you is you.

Your partner is not your family

On a very deep level, we get into relationships hoping that our partners will give us what our parents did not. We long for someone to show us unconditional love and acceptance, to really see us and understand us. We have been longing for it since we were children. Because of this desire to feel what we didn't get from our parents, we will subconsciously demand that our partners behave in ways that heal us. If they don't, we get completely triggered and wounded all over again. These are unfair demands.

These demands not being met is the number one reason why couples fight and break up. You entered into a relationship with unspoken requests and needs, and everyone gets upset when their partners let them down just like mommy and daddy did.

What is the alternative? We all have this lurking in our shadows. The first step is to shine a light on the shadow by being honest with yourself about what you are hoping your partner shows you or what you are hoping he heals for you. Then you need to realize that his job is NOT to heal you. Your job is NOT to heal him. You are both adults who need to take responsibility for your own needs and doing the necessary healing on your own so you can finally get over your childhood wounds already. I am not saying this lightly. I am quite serious, and I know it isn't that easy to just get over some of our painful pasts. However, if you want your partner to do the work to heal you, then you are setting yourself up to be re-wounded over and over. He will fail you at some point. That's not to say that healing won't spontaneously take place by being in and creating a healthy non-codependent relationship, but it cannot be the goal.

Mara was sobbing in my office because her husband had asked for a separation. She had regressed and looked like a sweet, heartbroken five-year-old. In fact, that is exactly what her brain was making her feel like. She had been abandoned by her father when she was four years old. Her mother had to go to work full time after her father left, and Mara was often left alone with neighbors who were strangers to her. She grew up lonely and isolated. Her secret hope when she met and married Brad was that he would ease her loneliness and she would finally have the family she always wanted.

Brad was going through a career shift. He was focusing all of his spare time on schoolwork and moving forward at his corporation. Mara was suffering because she felt abandoned. Her inner five-year-old was angry, sad and terrified that Brad was leaving her because of his new career passions. She had pushed so hard to get him to spend more time with her and was always upset every time he needed to study or stay late at work. Brad eventually asked for a separation because he felt he had to choose between something that was important to him and Mara's feelings. He chose himself. This was actually a healthy choice, but it sent Mara into a tailspin and flung her into the depth of her childhood wounds. When she began to explore her unspoken demands and the expectations she had been placing on Brad, she was able to see that he was not her father, and it wasn't his responsibility to give her everything that her father didn't. Their relationship began to heal when Mara realized that her husband's new career goals were his and they didn't have anything to do with her or him not wanting her. She began a journey to finally heal her past and took responsibility for being the one to do it. She reconciled with her husband, and because the pressure he felt from her was now gone, they were able to rekindle their love and both be partners and individuals.

10

Communication
"Asking for What You Want"

I n order to move successfully through the second and third trimesters of a relationship and beyond, it is imperative for couples to be able to communicate differences, upsets, desires and needs in a way that strengthens their relationships and not in a way that slowly deteriorates bonds and trust.

Most of the couples I work with that are on the brink of breaking up or are in conflict are having trouble communicating their needs in a way that their partners can really hear them and be inspired to honor requests. Most often the women complain that they don't feel understood or that their needs aren't getting met, and most men complain about feeling like they can't do anything right because their women are always complaining or upset. There is a major disconnect when it comes to men and women and the way they communicate with each other.

The differences boil down to this: Men are mono-focused problem solvers who want to provide. Women are not clear and direct with their needs, and often they don't feel like they have the right to have needs. As a result, their requests come out either murky or sounding like demands.

When women are with each other, they are empathic and caring and often don't need to be prompted to show love and emotional support when their girlfriends are in pain or experiencing problems. Men, on the other hand, are not as in touch with emotions— theirs or anyone else's. They are most often do-ers rather than feelers, and they look at the world and everything that comes their way as problems to solve, as I mentioned before.

So, when a woman comes to her man with an upset or an issue, his masculine brain kicks in with, "Awesome! A problem I can solve!" He wants his woman to be happy. He wants to provide for her, and problem-solving is one of the ways that he will try to do that.

This is a typical scene: you come home from a hard day at work after having had some conflict with your boss or co-worker. You begin to tell your guy about your day. You just want him to listen, understand and be compassionate. His masculine brain kicks in and he begins to discuss ways that you can fix your problem. You get annoyed because you don't want to talk about that; you just want empathy. You get frustrated with him for not listening to you, and then he shuts down because he has failed you. After all, he was only trying to help you because he wants you to be happy.

Women don't really have to be direct with their needs with other women in their lives, and they expect to communicate similarly with their men. Sadly, unless your man is psychic or a mind reader, this is not going to happen. Men just don't work that way.

Ways women miscommunicate to men

Women often don't feel comfortable asking for what they need. Historically, women have been the ones to put everyone else's needs first and have been taught to go without. We do still have needs and desires, of course, but it is harder for us to ask for them because we aren't used to recognizing their importance. Men, however, don't typically have a problem with having needs, nor do they have an issue with doing what they need to do to get them met. They expect their women to do the same. If you need something, your man will expect you to do what you need to get it or to be direct in asking for it.

Here are some typical things women do that DON'T get their needs met:

1. They drop hints. A woman won't come out directly and say what she wants, but rather hopes that her man picks up on the clues. She will often get frustrated and hurt when he doesn't understand what she is communicating, even though she is the one not being clear. She wants him to anticipate her needs without having to tell him.

2. They hold in their needs and frustrations to the point where they finally blow up like a volcano. When a woman erupts, completely blind-siding her man, he often goes into the defensive mode and gets angry back.

3. They manipulate the situation to get what they want, leaving their men feeling controlled and full of mistrust. Manipulation is just another method of indirect communication. Instead of just asking outright, a lot of strategizing and calculating goes into getting what you want.

4. They expect their men to know their wants and needs. When a woman's man fails to behave in the way she wants him to, she blames him for being insensitive and uncaring, when in reality he just doesn't know any better.

All of these scenarios leave men feeling shut down and defensive, which certainly doesn't lead to the women feeling understood and taken care of.

EXERCISE:
Needs

1. What are some of the needs and wants that you have had in the past that didn't get met in your relationships?

_____

_____

_____

_____

_____

2. How did you communicate your needs?

_____

_____

_____

_____

_____

3. How did you feel about not getting these needs met?

_____

_____

_____

_____

_____

4. How did you deal with not getting what you wanted?

_____

_____

_____

_____

_____

5. What were you assuming about the other person? In other words, what were you making it mean about you and him?

_____

_____

_____

_____

_____

Why Men LOVE a woman who is direct and honest

Men are linear thinkers. They really love a direct path from point A to point B. And when a woman communicates clearly what she wants and needs, a man's problem-solving brain gets very excited. Not only that but he sees that this is something he can "win" at, and he is more than happy to do something he can be successful at. In the first three trimesters of a relationship, men are evaluating the women they're dating to see if they will be their "forever" girls. One type of woman who they tend to look for is a low-drama woman who is in control of her emotions and doesn't blame other people for how she feels. Often, a woman who doesn't know how to do conflict resolution with a man will come off as a force to be reckoned with. She will blame him for making her feel terrible, and the first thing that a man will do at that point is feel like he is losing with her. If he loses more than he wins, he will eventually leave the relationship and you will not get through the stages to a committed relationship with him. And even if you do get to commit with him, if he feels like he can't make you happy he will eventually leave emotionally or physically.

A simple fix for the scenario above would look like this: you had a hard day at work. You come home and want to tell your partner about it so you can get it off your chest and move on after getting some comfort and reassurance. You already know that your man loves you so much that he would never want to see you in pain and that he'll want to fix it and problem solve it for you. You already know that isn't what you need. So, when you get home, you tell your partner, "I had a rough day at work. Is it okay if I share it with you really quick so I can move on? All I need is for you to listen and then give me a hug afterward. We don't need to solve anything. I just need to get this off my chest so I can enjoy the rest of the night with you."

He will be ecstatic that you just gave him the secret manual on how to win with you. You made it easy. You told him exactly what you wanted and needed, and he can't help but win. In his mind, he says to himself, "This is a low-drama woman who knows what she wants and makes it easy for me to make her happy."

The secret formula for getting your needs met without drama

It is funny that humans need to learn how to communicate properly. Most people don't know how to do this in a way that creates rapport and understanding. When they are in conflict, most people communicate in a way that escalates anger and misunderstanding. There are surefire ways to do this that will make your man want to listen and give you what you want. And there are surefire ways to create drama and a fight. All you need to do is make sure you don't put your guy on the defensive.

1. Mind-Set

Your state of mind is most important BEFORE you begin a critical conversation. If you are upset or angry it will come out in your tone, and your tone is more impactful than your words. The best frame of mind is a neutral feeling with a bit of curiosity. If you are upset, do something first to get yourself into a neutral state of mind. Seek to understand the situation or your guy and not to blame.

Also, make sure you are not already making any assumptions. Keep in mind that your guy really does want to make you happy and he is not your enemy. Remember, you do have a right to want what you want and have the needs that you have, but he doesn't HAVE to do what you want him to do. He has his own free will and so do you. Also, as we mentioned earlier, men are do-ers and not necessarily feelers. They need help recognizing feelings, so don't expect them to understand how you are feeling without telling them.

Getting clear with yourself first:

What is your intention for the conversation?
What do you want and need?
How are you feeling about not getting what you want and how would you feel
   if you did get your needs met?

2. Timing is EVERYTHING

A male brain is very mono-focused and can really only focus on one source of input at a time, unlike a female brain that can pay attention to many things at once, seeing all the parts and how they relate to the bigger picture.

If you are approaching your man to have an important conversation and he is in the middle of one of his focused linear cycles, he will not be able to give you his full attention. He needs to be able to finish what he is doing first so he can prepare to focus on you and the conversation. The best thing to do when approaching him to talk is to ask:

"Is this a good time to talk?" If he says, "yes," then go for it. If he says "no," then you can say, "Okay, when would be a good time to talk? I'm not upset, but I would like to talk to you about some things."

He will most likely tell you when a good time would be to come back for the conversation. Believe me, you really want him to be able to fully focus on you and what you have to say in order for this to go well. Letting him know you are not upset is a good thing because first, you won't be upset because you have first taken some time to get clear and calm. The worst thing a man can hear, the very words that send him into a panic, is this phrase from his lady, "We need to talk." All he can usually think of after that is that he is in trouble. Assuring him that this is not going to escalate into a dramatic scene helps him relax and helps ensure that he's in a good state of mind when you get to finally have the discussion.

3. Prime the positive well

So many men feel underappreciated. We as women are usually telling men what they are doing wrong, and not much energy is spent telling them what they are doing right. When he constantly hears what he is not doing right and rarely sees signs that you're happy, he will begin to feel like he is losing the relationship game and will eventually want to quit.

If you start the conversation off with what is going well or with a compliment or an appreciative comment about him, he will soften and feel more receptive to your request later. This is because he will feel like he is winning and will want to continue to win with you. For example, it might look like this:

"I want to really thank you for spending time with me on Sunday. I really enjoy our special time together." Or "I love how you picked the movie we saw last night with me in mind. I felt very special."

4. State your intention for the conversation (Keep it simple, one topic at a time)

Because men are straight line thinkers, if you state why you are having the conversation before you have it, his linear brain will relax because he will already know the purpose of the talk. Once he understands what you are trying to achieve, he can track what you are saying. Women often don't know what they want or aren't clear about why they are upset, and they feel like they need to justify why they are asking for what they are asking for, so they tend to go off on tangents or over-explain themselves. This is frustrating and confusing for the male brain who likes a direct path. Your man will most likely stop listening to you once he feels you are off track.

Stating the purpose or goal of the conversation might look like this:

"I am hoping to get clarity." or "I want to create more harmony or connection through this conversation."

This is where preparing for the conversation is very important. You need to get clear with your desires and goals before you bring it up to him or you will most likely not get what you are truly searching for.

5. State and observe the trigger situation or behavior

By this, I mean you should state a neutral observation about the particular behavior or situation that is bothering you. It is very important at this point to make sure you are objectively observing something clear and tangible WITHOUT judging the behavior. Once we use judging language, the natural reaction for your man will be to go into a defensive mode.

A neutral observation looks like this:

"When I see you looking at the computer screen while I'm telling you about my day…"

A judgment looks like this:

"When you ignore me when I am telling you about my day…"

Ignoring you is what you are making the behavior mean, but it isn't necessarily accurate. What is accurate is the behavior that triggers you—his looking at the computer screen when you are talking to him.

SHARE your emotions

Men need help understanding our emotions. When we are vulnerable and share ourselves and how we feel, they will soften and really understand WHY this is a problem. Because they do truly want to be the source of our happiness, they really get us when we share our emotions. We cannot expect them to guess how we feel at this point. And most likely a man wouldn't feel the same way as you do either.

This part is important to figure out before you have the conversation so you aren't tempted to use a judgment word disguised as a true emotion. For example, say, "I feel sad" versus "I am frustrated" or the ever popular, "I feel like you don't care." Saying "I am sad" is much more accurate and doesn't put the blame on your guy for how you are feeling. Saying "I am frustrated" or "I feel like you don't care" will immediately put him on the defensive because now you are judging him. The only option he has to not be seen as the bad guy is to defend himself.

Here are some feeling words that might occur when our needs are not being met:

Sad	Tired	Lonely
Puzzled	Embarrassed	Reluctant
Confused	Hopeless	Discouraged
Nervous	Disheartened	Angry
Concerned	Wary	Scared

Here are some judgment words disguised as feelings:

Ignored	Abandoned	Disrespected
Not important	Blamed	Attacked
Unheard	Unappreciated	Insulted
Misunderstood	Rejected	Neglected
Left out	Intimidated	Used

Once you figure out how you are really feeling without judgment words, it is also a good idea to figure out how you would rather be feeling. Don't worry. We will start to put this all together soon so it will make sense.

Here are some feeling words when our needs ARE being met:

Happy	Connected	Confident
Hopeful	Fulfilled	Relieved
Grateful	Joyful	Trustful
Inspired	Safe	Proud
Optimistic	Eager	Glad

6. Request versus demand

There is a big difference between a request and a demand. A request implies that someone always has the option to say "no." On our end we need to be okay with that. We can't be attached to an outcome. This is a dialogue between you and your partner, not a time for you to strong-arm your guy into doing your bidding.

A request looks like this:

"Would you be willing to...?"

A demand looks like this:

"I want you to…" or "You need to…"

When you make a request of your partner, he will feel in control. Nobody likes feeling pushed to do something against his will. People are more likely to want to be collaborative instead of resistant when they have options and don't feel backed into a corner.

The biggest thing to remember if your man says "no" to your request is not to make it mean anything about you. Often this is where our limiting beliefs can rear their ugly heads and get us triggered or back in the hurt space of "he doesn't care about me." It isn't about you; it is about him. There might be many reasons why he says "no" in response to what you want or need. This is a great opportunity to ask him if he would be willing to share why he doesn't want to do what you are asking and then ask if he can offer another solution. This really helps a man feel in control and gets his problem-solving juices flowing. And his "no" doesn't mean that you cannot still get what you want or need. It means that there needs to be a collaboration and discussion of how that can happen in a way that works for both people.

You are in control of your happiness. If your guy says "no" to something that is a deal breaker for you and there is no way to resolve the issue, this is not the time to try to convince him to change. It is your job to communicate clearly, and if there is no solution then it is also your job to decide if this is something you can live with because you will NEVER change him. If it is something you can't live with, then it is also your job to decide if you will stay or leave.

Helping your man FEEL

Often men haven't had the freedom to really learn how to express their emotions. Sadly, a lot of men just comply with women's wishes because they have been taught that they shouldn't disagree. You don't want to have a "must please Mommy" syndrome on your hands. It might be good practice to make sure your guy is really on board with whatever gets agreed upon.

Example:
"How do you feel about me asking you for this?"

Asking him this will also ensure that he isn't just saying "yes" to comply, and it offers him space to really express himself, which he will be grateful for. In addition, you won't get into a situation where he says he will do something and then passively aggressively doesn't do it because he wasn't really on board.

Putting the formula together

I know that this might be a new way of looking at communication, and it might seem confusing at first. It does take practice. Don't feel weird about practicing or writing things out in the beginning to help you get the hang of it.

Here is the simple formula laid out:

Mindset

Do this before you have the conversation. Decide how you are feeling without judgment words. Also, figure out how you would like to feel instead. Get clear about your intentions for the conversation and what you would like the outcome to be.

Timing is everything

"Is this a good time to talk?"

If he says, "no," you then say, *"Okay, when would be a better time for you? I am not upset; I just want to discuss some things with you."*

Prime the positive well

"When we had the picnic on the beach last week, I felt so seen and close to you. That was amazing."

Observe the trigger behavior without judgment

"When I come home and haven't seen you all day, I really want to be able to connect with you. I feel sad when I come home and start to talk to you about my day and you are looking at the computer screen."

Request

"Would you be willing to close your computer when I get home so we can re-connect?"

Him: *"Well, what if I'm in the middle of something important and I can't just stop what I'm doing?"*

You: *"Okay, I get it. So how else can we re-connect at the end of the day?"*

Him: *"What if when you get home, I will stop what I am doing and give you a hug. If I can stop what I am doing right then, I will. If I can't, I will tell you how long I'll need before I can pay attention to you. But regardless, I will always stop and hug you when you walk in the door. Will that work?"*

Ask how he feels

You: *"How do you feel about me asking this of you?"*

Stop talking at that point and just listen. Remember, the masculine brain needs a little bit of time to process emotions, so be silent until he answers.

11

The Feminine and Masculine Dance of Relationships

The concept of masculine and feminine energy and roles in relationship and society is a hot button topic. It is also an important topic to cover when discussing the new paradigm of intimate relationships. It is a topic that is newly being explored, and being able to grasp the concepts will help you create a long-lasting passion in your dating and love relationships. The women who get upset by this conversation often have a misperception of feminine energy as being weak and subservient. When I suggest that they tap into their feminine energy when dating, they often think I am telling them to become submissive. This is far from the truth and feminine energy is far from weak. Let's just start the conversation with the ideas that:

1. You have both masculine and feminine energy inside of you.
2. The energies are completely equal and valuable.
3. Though equal, they are very different.
4. The polarity of both energies inside of you and in an intimate relationship is juicy.

I use the terms feminine and masculine energy when talking about these concepts. Energy is hard to describe with words. It isn't something you can visually see. It is something deeper and more detectable with a felt sense, hence making it a challenging topic to teach and explain. Remember this topic is huge so I will only be able to touch on some of the basic concepts. However, it is a very necessary topic when revamping the way women have been participating in relationships that have left them feeling frustrated and unfulfilled. If both men and women are able to harness these energies and know when to play with them in their relationships, they will be able to create passion and juiciness that will sustain them for the duration. We will begin by giving some examples of the different energies that each hold.

Masculine energy:

1. Linear thinking
2. Going from point A to Point B
3. Directive
4. Felt in the head—thinking
5. Dominant
6. Getting sh#@ done
7. Stiff, tense and angular body

Here is an example of a masculine energy day:

You have a meeting at work with the boss and your team today. You wake up in the morning, quickly shower and get dressed without much thought. You still make sure you look nice, but your attention is focused on the upcoming meeting. You are in your head rehearsing your presentation. You leave the house in a rush and walk to the subway. You are doing the urban power walk, and without breaking your stride, you catch the train just in time. You get to work, look over your notes and head to the conference room. Your voice is unwavering and strong. You are on point. You feel powerful and influential. Your team and your boss are impressed. After the meeting, you stop by the dry cleaners to pick up your dress suit. You grab a sandwich and eat it while you are walking down the street toward the cleaners. You head back to work to finish up some paperwork and then leave right at 4:30 to make sure you can catch the train back in time to pick up your dog at doggie daycare before they close. You arrive home, fix dinner, wash the dishes and go to bed.

As you can see, this kind of energy stays on task, is goal-oriented and more in the head than in the body. It is fast and focused energy. This is a get S*#& done kind of day.

Feminine energy:

1. Multi-tasking
2. Non-direct path
3. Passive and receptive
4. Felt in the body—slower
5. Getting stuff done with flow
6. Creative
7. Soft, supple and relaxed body

Here is an example of a feminine energy kind of day:

You and one of your girlfriends decide to go away on a spa retreat. You show up to the hotel that is surrounded by meadows and beautiful rolling hills. Before going up to check into the hotel, you stop to smell the crisp air and watch the hummingbirds circle around. Your body is already feeling the relaxation of being on vacation. You slowly walk up the stairs to your room and gently put your suitcase down on the bed.

You and your girlfriend proceed to take a long, slow walk up to the hot tubs and stop along the way to smell the flowers and watch the squirrels chasing each other. You soak next to your friend while reading a book. When dinnertime comes your friend suggests that you go to the restaurant on the grounds and then bring the food out into the garden to eat. You are fine with her choice and happy to lean back and enjoy yourself without having to make too many decisions.

As you can see, this kind of day is slower and more relaxed. Things still get accomplished but with more flow instead of a direct path. Attention is paid to the senses and slowing down to enjoy experiences fully. It is a sensual experience and more body-oriented than thinking-oriented.

The difference between roles and energy

Historically, there have been women's roles and men's roles. This is where the feminine/masculine conversation usually goes off track because women don't want to be thrown back into repressive, antiquated roles. When we are talking about the different energies, we are not talking about roles. In fact, some of the traditional female roles required considerable masculine energy. For example, a woman traditionally being the primary caretaker of the children and household manager required an insane amount of focus, direction, and task-oriented energy, going from point A to point B to get everything taken care of. In this sense, masculine energy was essentially needed to accomplish this even though it was a traditionally feminine role. Also, the traditional, stereotypical image of the man coming home from work and sitting on the couch with his cocktail in hand all slumped down and relaxed with his mind turned off was the feminine energy of flow and body. So that said, let's throw the old roles out. They will not be useful in today's conversation.

Everyone has both energies

All men and all women have access to both energies inside of them. We also have one energy that dominates our true sexual essence, meaning the one that we prefer in sexual, intimate relationships. Even though we can and do play out both energies in our relationships, it is the one energy you like to be in or prefer that turns us on or creates a spark. Most women have a true feminine sexual essence and most men have a true masculine sexual essence; however, there are some women who have a true masculine essence and vice versa.

A question to ask yourself to find this out for yourself is, "Where do you get energized and fed?" For instance, when I am in launch mode for the relationship courses that I facilitate, and I have to go to meetings, teach and even when writing this book, I can get jazzed up. But if I keep up that high-intensity, fast, directive energy without a break, I will get burned out because masculine energy isn't my true essence. I love my masculine energy and it can really get sh#@ done. But if I don't spend some time in my feminine energy, I feel depleted. My feminine energy might look like going to a yoga class and spending some quality time with a close girlfriend while really connecting with her. It might be taking a long, luxurious bath, drawing, painting or walking in nature. Someone who has a true masculine essence would get very energized by moving things forward and going from point A to point B and taking charge. On the other hand, I see a lot of men stuck these days because they lack access to their true masculine energy. If a true masculine is lacking direction or purpose in his life, he will end up feeling empty and depressed.

I think of masculine energy as being like the river banks and feminine energy being the river. The river has flow and is powerful but without the container of the banks it would spill out everywhere and not have any direction. It is important to develop both energies within yourself. You need your inner masculine energy to go out there and make things happen. You need to work and pay the bills, and you need to have a container around your feminine so you aren't relying solely on others to contain you. But you also need to have the flow of the feminine or else you become just a dried-up river bed.

Not only that, but feminine energy is the number one thing that attracts a masculine man. And by masculine, I mean a man who has direction and purpose, and who makes us swoon.

Think of masculine and feminine attraction like a magnet. When two opposite sides of the magnet face each other, they attract each other and pull together. But when two of the same sides face each other, they repel each other. If you are in your masculine energy then you will repel your man's masculine energy. Either you will polarize him to be more in his feminine or you will butt heads or your energy will take on the feel of business partners, collaborating and neutral instead of lover energy. All of these are fine. It is all about what you want. Sexual spark and chemistry and juiciness is created by differences and is really yummy when each person is in an opposite energy. It is fun to play around with both energies on occasion in a sexual interaction. However, most women I know have a true feminine sexual essence and, therefore, really swoon when a man has direction, makes plans and lets her relax into the moment.

EXERCISE:
Relationship with your energies

What is your relationship with your feminine energy? What do you believe about feminine energy?

_____

_____

_____

_____

_____

What is your relationship with your masculine energy? What do you believe about masculine energy?

_____

_____

_____

_____

_____

The feminist revolution

Since the dawn of the feminist movement, both men and women have been disowning core pieces of themselves. Women stepped into the work world and had to start competing with men in the world. In doing so, they began rejecting their own feminine sides. Since that time, men, have also cut off their masculine essence, basically because they became afraid of women's wrath. Women were pissed off and very anti-men. In reality, though, they were fighting against toxic masculinity that had been oppressing them. True masculine energy is not oppressive. We will talk more about toxic feminine and toxic masculine energies and how they play out.

The sexual revolution needed to happen. Equality is important. The sexual revolution got us more equality, but it was not in favor of the feminine. Women bought into the lie that feminine energy was weak and so they threw it out for the sake of equality. The feminist revolution was the most anti-feminine thing to happen to us. As the dust settles, we are now seeing that the disenfranchised sense of our own feminine essences is literally killing us. Women are stressed, overwhelmed and confused as to why their relationships are flaccid. They long for deep, passionate lives and experiences in love, and are sorely disappointed that they are not getting what they want.

Disowning their feminine energy and not allowing themselves to drop into that energy in their relationships or at other times in their lives is the main culprit of their dissatisfaction.

The challenge is this modern world in which women have become very self-sufficient. We are great at multi-tasking and getting things done, and we are powerhouses of energy in the work world. Setting goals, direction, execution and planning all require our masculine energy. And women can do all of that quite well. The sad thing is that running masculine energy all the time in our lives without balancing it by letting our feminine energy shine as well will always take a toll on us. Because masculine energy is not our true energy, it drains us. Men, on the other hand, whose natural essence is usually masculine, will be recharged and rejuvenated by having direction, planning and executing. The problem, though, is that the world requires masculine energy for survival. It is not optional. Feminine energy, which is not required for survival, ends up getting pushed to the back burner, upsetting the balance necessary for a healthy dynamic

Let's face it. Going to work, paying the bills, riding the subway, driving in traffic, and meeting deadlines all require the masculine force of direction and planning. However, women these days are finding that their developed skills of conducting business in the world are also displacing the men in their lives with regards to their masculinity. This is resulting in flaccid relationships without much passion and is also causing women to complain that they don't feel desired, cherished or cared for. What men really want and need to be able to step into their own masculinity is to be able to take charge, plan for our happiness and protect us. Masculine traits are driven by direction, planning and focusing on goals. Women have gotten so good at this in their own day-to-day lives that they forget to hang up their masculine hats when they come home to their partners. They start directing their relationships and even worse, directing their men. The men I work with often complain that they feel emasculated in their relationships. This chronic masculine energy that she is in is taking a toll not only in the romance department but also in the bedroom. Their passion for their ladies tends to dwindle as they get overwhelmed by their women planning everything and not really letting them have any control. They also feel that they don't have anything to offer women who have their lives so perfectly mapped out. Unfortunately for us women, masculine energy is required for survival. And feminine energy is a nice touch but not necessary to get by in the world. Most women need to turn on their masculine energy every day when they leave the house, and not only is it difficult to turn it off when you come home but quite often women have no idea what feminine energy is, nor have they ever had the opportunity to develop it for themselves. Worse yet, some women look at feminine energy as being weak and powerless and end up rejecting it altogether.

Most of the women I work with need to learn how to receive love and care from a man and are often blocked by limiting beliefs of their own self-worth. Many are also blocked by childhood traumas that impact their ability to trust people or cause them not to feel safe being vulnerable around a man. In order to allow your man to step up and plan things or give to you, to embrace him in his masculine and yourself in your feminine, you need to be able to trust him.

Here are a few questions to ask yourself to see if you might be using a lot of masculine energy in your relationship:

1. Do you feel the need to plan everything in your relationship? If so why?

2. Do you give your partner space to make plans for the both of you?

3. If your man plans something, do you happily follow his lead? Or do you need to control the situation?

4. Do you feel like you need to control your partner?

5. Do you feel relaxed and trusting around your guy?

6. Are you able to relax and surrender to his direction?

7. Are you able to be open and vulnerable around him?

8. Do you nag him to do things or do you ask for things lovingly, trusting that he wants to make you happy and is not your enemy?

9. Do you feel like you fully open your heart to him? Or are there barriers blocking you?

The ultimate quality of feminine energy is *love* itself. It is open, loving, caring, trusting and flowing. Masculine energy is the container that surrounds the feminine and protects her and guides her through life. Both energies are needed in yourself and in a relationship to keep the passion and excitement. They are both equal and also very different. In the past, before the sexual revolution, feminine energy was considered less than equal. But as the dust settles since the sixties, it is becoming apparent that both energies are necessary for healthy, thriving relationships. It is a difficult task to return to our feminine and cultivate it so that it becomes natural to us. Because most women have a natural true feminine essence, we are doing ourselves a disservice in suppressing it.

One of the mistakes that a woman often makes with her man is that she is always DOING things to try and make him appreciate her and love her more. There she is cooking, cleaning, planning dates, etc. But she doesn't seem to get the attention that she wants from her guy, no matter how hard she tries. Sadly, what she doesn't know is that everything she is DOING actually requires masculine energy, and she is unknowingly repelling her guy the more she *does*. Not that he doesn't appreciate it, but it doesn't ATTRACT him like she is hoping it will. The core essence of the feminine that attracts the masculine is radiance.

Radiance is not a doing but it is a BEING. Being fully relaxed, creative and rejuvenated is when your feminine essence can shine. When you are fully relaxed and in your body, you can be open, vulnerable, loving and playful, which is the radiance and feminine energy that turns men on the most.

If you are not doing things to recharge yourself every day from running around in a masculine world, you will become stressed and burned out. You will not be playful or open or vulnerable. You will be irritated, closed, resentful and bitter. This is the opposite of feminine radiance.

The best way to cultivate this feminine energy is by doing extreme self-care. A woman's main priority should be on her own self-care, rejuvenation and pleasure. When she puts herself first in this way, she will begin to shine, and her man will also put her as his priority. Feminine radiance is so powerful that it draws a man in like a moth to a flame and all he wants to do is bask in your light.

It might seem difficult and selfish to put yourself first, but believe me, if you are cultivating your own interests and making your life as juicy as it can be, you will actually be benefiting everyone around you, including your guy. Remember, men just want the women they are with to be happy. And when you are happy and passionate in your life, it will make him feel awesome and he will want to be around that kind of energy. Think of what it is like to be around someone who is tired, stressed, bored or irritable. No fun, right? Now imagine being around someone who is full of life, happy and light. You want to be around them more! I am not saying that you can't ever be stressed or upset. We are all human and having a bad day is normal. I am talking about your constant and default state.

Why do women disown their feminine?

Many women have a negative relationship with feminine energy. They reject it and try to stay away from it as much as possible. Why would someone disown a part of herself that is so beautiful and necessary to feel balanced and whole?

Abuse and trauma

Feminine energy lives in the body, senses, feeling and emotions, while masculine energy lives in the mind and thinking. Some women have a difficult time connecting with their bodies due to past sexual trauma or physical assault or even the fear of the potential threat of sexual assault. If a woman has been sexually abused in some way, abandoning the body by escaping into the mind is a great survival technique. She might feel that it was her body that got her in trouble in the first place, so disowning it makes sense in order to stay safe. If you have abuse in your past, I recommend doing some sort of therapy to unwire that safety patterning so that being in your feminine energy and your body is safer for you. The clients who I work with around unwiring trauma become more and more open to feeling safe and to being more vulnerable, which allows them the deeper connections and intimacy that they are craving in their love lives.

Growing up on your own

When children grow up in households that are abusive or neglectful in some way or they feel like they need to take care of themselves—either because the parents aren't paying attention to them or even just seem to not be—they can have an overdeveloped sense of responsibility and need for control. Those children will learn that survival is up to them and that they can't rely on anyone else. Their feminine energies of feeling, playfulness, flow and creativity were not the aspects that would have gotten them through those experiences. So when it comes to surrendering control or allowing their men to take charge, this might trigger a fear response so deeply that they need to be in their masculine energy of doing and planning in order to feel like they can survive.

In order to be in your receptive feminine energy and let someone else play the masculine role, you need to be able to give up control. You need to be able to trust that the other person will be able to follow through and not hurt you. Surrender takes extreme trust.

Boys and girls

In some families, boys are more valued than girls. Not only that but often, the things that children get praised for are their masculine energy achievements. They get praise for getting things done and for being on task. Their more playful creative sides often get ignored. In families where attention and love feel conditional, the children might start disowning the things in themselves that don't get valued by their parents and start to cultivate more of the traits that they see their parents valuing. Thus, they will disown pieces of themselves in order to be loved.

What does it feel like to give up control?

Feeling in control can make us feel safe. When outcomes and life seem predictable, then we feel more secure. But if you're controlling your relationships and your partners in an effort to feel secure and safe, you not only run the risk of driving your man away, but you cannot have a strong, protective, directive masculine man in your life either. You might even be polarizing your man to be more flowy and directionless if he lets you do everything because you need to be the one in control. If you find that you have a hard time giving up control and trusting other people to take care of things, it's likely that you do not trust yourself. If you did, you would know that if someone didn't pull through or they failed you somehow or broke your heart, that your own masculine energy could swoop in and take care of your feminine self. If you trust yourself, you can also trust others more easily. It isn't as risky when you know that you can step in to protect yourself when necessary instead of being on constant guard. If you are in constant protection mode, you cannot fully feel your open, loving, beautiful feminine essence. It is good to know that you can take care of yourself. But do you really want to have to take care of yourself all the time?

Feminine strength

Often women will disown their feminine essence because they have a misperception that it is weak. They might feel as if it is submissive and powerless. Often the powerhouse women I meet are afraid that if they embrace their feminine essence, they won't be able to get ahead in the world. The world of power and business tends to be masculine, and masculine energy is rewarded and praised. It is true that feminine power is different than masculine power. Feminine power is not weak—not by far. It is just a different kind of strong. It is helpful to be able to harness both kinds of power as well as the ability to switch on the energy that will help you out the most, depending on the situation. Yes, maybe masculine power will be good when getting a project done at work; however, feminine power might be appropriate when you need to lead a team or group, helping them all feel understood and facilitating connection.

Masculine energy leads with the mind and doesn't often look at the whole. Rather it looks at single steps. In contrast, feminine energy leads with the heart, focuses on connection and can see the bigger picture more often than masculine leadership.

In love relationships, the feminine strength and gifts to the masculine are to be a pathway to emotions and vulnerability. When a woman who is embodied with compassionate and loving energy and a peaceful mind walks into the room, you bet she affects the people around her. When you are powerful in your true feminine essence, you encourage others to be big, open and vulnerable, and you give them permission to shine as well.

It's wonderful for women to also feel free to be in their masculine energy. The problem is when both men and women feel shame around their feminine side because it is considered, "less than" by society. The old feminism has not healed the shame around being feminine but instead won the freedom for women to be more masculine. I see a particularly damaging aspect to this in that women are determined to show their value by being busy, non-receptive, unfeeling and productive (all masculine traits).

Toxic femininity

As I mentioned before, feminine essence at its core is just love. The feminine desires love, beauty, and connection. However, it can get toxic when she looks for these things outside of herself—when she doesn't feel love unless she is being loved by someone else, if she only acknowledges her beauty and brightness when she is being adored by someone else. When she looks for her value in the reflection of a lover, this is what I call *toxic feminine energy*. It's impossible to love too much when love is healthy and given freely on both sides. It is unhealthy when love is given only as a way to get love back. Often when someone is experiencing toxic feminine energy, she will give and give in order to get love back. Or she will twist and morph herself, trying to be what she thinks her lover wants in order to get love. She fails to see that in her trueness she, the feminine is already all that is love. You need nothing except for the ability to feel this trueness in yourself.

When you can do this then you will be free to give love and to receive it in a healthy and clean way.

Ask yourself, "When in the past has my feminine energy been toxic?"

Toxic masculinity

Toxic masculine energy is loud, brash, manipulative, and controlling. It is all that we see that is corrupt in politics and in the violence in the world. It is not true masculine energy; it is posturing that is designed to cover up insecurity and fear.

When is your masculine toxic?

It could look like those times where you are feeling out of control and you are yelling or pushing someone around in order to get your way or to take back some kind of power. It emerges when you are feeling afraid or insecure and not really feeling powerful. It is a posturing of power.

The new masculine and the new feminine

As people start to pay more and more attention to these concepts, I am hoping that the new masculine and new feminine evolve within all people. The ultimate goal is a world in which everyone is comfortable with both of their energies and can have full access to all of themselves, where men can be emotional and present as well as go-getters, and where women can kick ass in the world but not at the expense of their softer, creative, emotive sides. When women and men can become whole, our relationships will flourish.

How to handle male privilege in dating

Have you ever had this frustrating dating experience? There you are on a first date with a man. Time to get to know each other, right? Time to build a connection to see if you want to take it to the next level. Time to see if there is chemistry.

Then it goes like this:

Woman: asks the man a question to get to know him better

Man: answers question

Woman: waits for the man to ask her a question back

Man: keeps talking about himself

Woman: asks more questions hoping and waiting for him to ask her back so he can get to know her too

Man: keeps talking about himself and keeps talking and keeps talking
The date is over. "Thank Gawd!"

Man: "Hey, it was great meeting you. I had fun. Let's get go out again."

Woman: Thinks to herself: "Of course you had fun. You got to blab on about yourself all night and be listened to. Stupid blankity blank."

She leaves the date realizing that he doesn't know anything more about her than he did before the date. She feels unvalued, unseen, frustrated, and most likely drained by the unequal exchange of energy that just ensued.

Annoying, right? Most women who have dated men have had one or more experiences like this.

In the past, I have made this mean a few things:

1. The man is self-absorbed and full of himself.
2. He is a social idiot.
3. His mother didn't raise him right.

The latter is probably most true. Women's rights have come a long way, but what still lurks in the shadows is male privilege. Privilege is a special right, advantage or immunity granted or available only to a particular person or a group of people. The kicker about privilege is that men often don't even know or see the ways that they are putting women off. If you ask most men, they will say that they respect and value women. They will be all for equal rights. However, the dark side of patriarchy has infiltrated deep and is still present in harder-to-detect ways. Society has trained men without them even knowing it to feel like they have certain rights to take up space, talk over people and dominate conversations, and that their opinions absolutely NEED to be heard. Women have also been unknowingly perpetuating this paradigm. No one is innocent here. As young girls, we were trained to listen to men just because they are men. We have watched our mothers cater to our fathers, usually at their own expense and happiness. We watched those same mothers treat their male children differently than their girls, doting on the boys and requiring less from them. Then girls go to school where this dynamic is reinforced, quite often by female teachers. The boys get called on more often and if they are loud and disruptive, they are just boisterous and being boys. When a girl speaks out and is strong or loud, she is out of line and given less leeway. Boys who speak out are seen as leaders. Girls who are equally outspoken are seen as bossy.

The list can go on. Really, I am not complaining here, mostly because complaining just makes you a victim. What I am saying though is this: as women, we need to take responsibility for our own insidious behavior and stop perpetuating male privilege. Most men don't even realize they are advantaged. Life has always just been that way for them so they have big blind spots when it comes to seeing it play out.

Fortunately, there are some more enlightened men who try to change the subtle or not so subtle ways that they might have been behaving to overshadow women. However, if we leave it up to men to correct the imbalance, it might not happen. Often, they don't see it. And how can you change something you don't see? The big question is: As a woman, how have you been feeding into the inequality between the sexes?

Throughout history, men have been accustomed to women putting them first and making them a priority while they get to go focus on their own lives, jobs, passions, hobbies, etc. and then get to come back to a doting supportive woman. Said woman most likely has also been focusing on HIS life, passions, hobbies, etc. Men have been used to women making things easy for them by being available, sacrificing and accommodating. We have been trained to stay quiet when a man is dominating the conversation. If he gets louder and interrupts, we mostly just take it and shut up because it feels strangely rude to try to push our way into a conversation to be heard. In "woman land" the rules are politer. We tend to be conscientious of stage time when we are speaking. We ask questions and we listen. When we are out with our girlfriends, we make sure we aren't taking control over what is happening, we make sure everyone is being heard and we pay attention to everyone's needs, not just our own. Quite often when we are with men, we continue "woman land" rules. We coddle them, listen to them, don't interrupt them, make them a priority and give up things for them. They don't even notice what we are doing for them because it has always been like that for them everywhere they go.

So, my beautiful sisters, if we want this dynamic to finally stop, then we have to stop playing the role that got us here in the first place. It might mean that when a man is dominating the conversation that we interject and point it out to him. "Hey, what you're talking about is interesting but I haven't been able to join the conversation, and I feel like I am just being talked at."

It might look like this: When a man interrupts you, you calmly inform him that he just interrupted you, and you would like to finish what you were saying. Then you actually continue what you were saying as if nothing just derailed you. It might mean that you stop putting your man or relationship first. What if you go out into the world and focus on your life, your career, your friends and things that make YOU happy, while at the same time assuming that your man will be there waiting for you when you come back home? In other words, what if you didn't feel the need to keep feeding the relationship all of your energy and you can still trust that he isn't going anywhere? What if you and what you want becomes your priority? I'm not saying your relationship isn't important, but what if it actually came second to your own life? Your man might have to get used to not being the center of your world and the center of the universe as he has so sadly been taught is his right.

The other big behavioral shift is to stop waiting for a man to choose you. So many women walk around in the world with the mindset that they are hoping a man will pick them. This feeds right into the outdated male-centric society in which the men have all of the control. It also plays into the idea that men are owed a girlfriend no matter what kind of effort they put in (or don't) or how much of a catch they are themselves.

Not only is it good for the budding relationship for a man to win a woman over, but if you become the chooser, you begin to break the shackles of history that required women to bend over backwards to entice a man. You are already a catch. Stop chasing him. Stop making it so easy. I am not saying playing hard to get is the answer. After breaking it down, it is actually a simple mindset shift. "Instead of asking, "Am I what he wants?" ask yourself, "Is he what I want?"

I am not a man hater. I love men (well, most men that is) and sometimes they frustrate me. I have many amazing men in my life who treat women equally and make sure that they aren't dominating them. I also realize that men have had their own challenges when it comes to revamping masculinity into something that isn't toxic and still being able to be powerful in their own lives. What I am saying is that we, as women, need to change things for **us**. We aren't here to teach men anything. I am also not saying that men don't need to take responsibility for themselves in this matter and that it is up to us alone. But we need things to be better for us. We need things to be better for our relationships and for our daughters. And actually, when we stop catering to men it will be better for them too. If we wait for men to fix this then we are just perpetuating our powerlessness. It is time for the new masculine and the new feminine to emerge.

How to foster your feminine energy

The feminine essence resides in the body. Anything that you can do to get you into your body will help you begin to rejuvenate and activate the feminine. We tend to live in our heads. We are either planning the future, regretting the past or analyzing the present. This mental activity takes us out of the present moment and out of the sensations and sensuality of being in the body. Most activities such as meditation, yoga or dancing will bring you into your body and there you will find joy. The masculine lives in the mind and uses the body as a tool. For the feminine, the body is her temple and where she finds her true self.

EXERCISE:
List some activities that bring you into your body

_____

_____

Some examples might include soaking in a hot tub, taking a sauna, yoga, dance, embodied sex, massage, meditation or taking a bath. I recommend doing one of these things every day to reconnect with your feminine because masculine activities will drain you. You will need to recharge after a masculine energy day. It might be especially necessary to do one of these things before you go out on a date or spend time with your partner so you can drop into this energy before you meet.

Feminine energy has been my best friend and my continual struggle

Up until recently, I wouldn't have been able to even tell you what feminine energy felt like. I was one of those women who felt like I was in competition with men and never wanted to seem weak. I was a go-getter my whole life and didn't really appreciate women or feminine energy for most of my life, let alone even know there was a difference.

Unfortunately, it took a series of unpleasant events to wake me up to what I was manifesting in my life. My first wakeup call was that I hit a level of adrenal exhaustion that put me in bed for almost a month. High levels of stress, excitement, turbulent relationships, forging forward in my career and pushing myself without rest had taken its toll. My body had had enough and it was going to force me to slow down. I had no choice but to figure out how to balance my life and turn on some rejuvenating feminine energy or I was never going to get better. I realized that my go-getter energy was rooted in a couple of things. First, I was raised in the Midwest and came from Dutch farmers.

My people and my neighbors all worked hard. Enjoying life was not a priority. And even though I had moved to California and thought I was living a holistic, balanced, hippie, Californian lifestyle, my upbringing was still pushing me harder than I could manage.

The second unfortunate event that woke me up to my over-running masculine energy was my marriage and divorce. In my marriage, I became painfully aware that I had once again attracted a man who had weak masculine energy, meaning he didn't have purpose or direction and was lost. He looked toward me to guide everything in the relationship from vacations to his career to whether or not we were going to move or if the dog needed a walk. After my divorce, I had to take a long look at what I had been doing to call these kinds of men into my life. My former husband was not the first man in my life who relied heavily on me for direction. I was resentful and just wanted to have someone who I could rely on for a change.

The reason these men kept showing up all came back to my prevalent masculine energy. I am amazing at planning and organizing and getting things done. I don't sit still for very long and this had all come out in my love life as well.

In the vain of polarity, men who were not as strong in their own masculine energy were attracted to me. And I had to be honest—subconsciously, I was attracted to them because they were going to let me be in control. The other root of my issue was because of my traumatic childhood, I was one of those people who didn't trust others to take care of things and especially not to take care of me. It was better for me to be the one to do it myself. Picking men who would let me take charge suited my issues. However, I would constantly complain that I was always the one who had to take care of things. My rigid masculine energy made sensuality and sex not as juicy. There was passion missing from a lot of my past relationships and I had a deep longing to surrender to someone and fall deeply. I kept telling myself that I hadn't yet met a man who was capable of doing this for me and that I just needed to find a strong man—someone stronger than me who I could trust. That might have been true, but what was also true was that I wasn't going to let anyone take the lead or let myself surrender. I knew that if I wanted to be fulfilled in love, I needed to work this out. I needed to be able to step back and let someone lead. I needed to learn how to trust.

Fortunately, because of my awesome masculine energy, when I set out to do something it happens. After my divorce, I put myself to the task of learning how to switch on my feminine energy. I practiced embodiment. I practiced dating and letting men pursue me. I practiced letting them make plans and being happy with whatever they came up with. I did daily body practices to shut off my mind and get more in my feminine body, including, yoga, art and baths.

I am happy to say that all of this work and attention has paid off. My current boyfriend is an amazing leader. I am not sure if he always was or if I just created the space for him to step up. We both seem to be able to play in our masculine and feminine energies together and there is a juicy polarity and chemistry between us because of it. This is the first relationship I have been in where I let go and trust that he will do things. It is absolutely beautiful and because of it, I get to be in my loving, vulnerable self.

If you think it is too difficult to change something, please know that anything you put your mind to can happen. And if you have been frustrated with the men in your life not stepping up, then instead of wanting them to be different, I encourage you to look at what energy you might be bringing to the table and ask yourself what do you really want? And what energy will create that?

Resources

For more information about the F.L.I.R.T. dating and relationship courses and your free audio course, "3 Big Mistakes that are Keeping You Alone." please visit:

www.myinspiring-love.com

For more information about deep transformational N.L.P. neuro re-patterning please visit.

www.cinthiadennis.com

If you live in the San Francisco Bay area and would like to be invited to workshops and events, please contact Cinthia at cinthiadennis@gmail.com to be added to her invite list.

About the Author

Cinthia Dennis, MA Human Development and Transformational N.L.P., has been teaching and facilitating relationship and dating courses as well as helping countless men and women remove deep blocks keeping them from the lives they are meant to live since 2005. She is an inspirational speaker and teacher, artist, writer and lover of the human experience.

Made in the USA
Lexington, KY
18 May 2019